THE COLLEGE ADVENTURE HANDBOOK

THE ULTIMATE GUIDE FOR SURVIVING COLLEGE, BUILDING A STRONG FAITH, AND GETTING A HOT DATE

ROB STENNETT AND JOE KIRKENDALL

THE
COLLEGE
ADVENTURE
HANDBOOK

THE ULTIMATE GUIDE FOR SURVIVING COLLEGE, BUILDING A STRONG FAITH, AND GETTING A HOT DATE

ROB STENNETT AND JOE KIRKENDALL

youth specialties

ZONDERVAN.com/
AUTHORTRACKER
follow your favorite authors

ZONDERVAN

The College Adventure Handbook

Copyright © 2011 by Rob Stennett and Joseph P. Kirkendall III

YS Youth Specialties is a trademark of YOUTHWORKS!, INCORPORATED and is registered with the United States Patent and Trademark Office.

This title is also available as a Zondervan ebook.
Visit www.zondervan.com/ebooks

Requests for information should be addressed to:

Zondervan, Grand Rapids, Michigan 49530

Library of Congress Cataloging-in-Publication Data

Stennett, Rob, 1977
    The college adventure handbook : the ultimate guide for surviving
college, building a strong faith, and getting a hot date / Rob Stennett and Joe
Kirkendall.
    p. cm.
    ISBN 978-0-310-67085-8
    1. Christian college students—Religious life. 2. College student orientation.
I. Kirkendall, Joe. II. Title..
BV4531.3.S75 2010
248.8'34—dc22   2010037699

Cover design: Toolbox Studios
Interior design: David Conn

Printed in the United States of America

11 12 13 14 /DCI/ 20 19 18 17 16 15 14 13 12 11 10 9 8 7 6 5 4 3 2

CONTENTS

PART 4 (DANGEROUS SITUATIONS)

PART 5 (ELECTIVES)

THIS BOOK IS

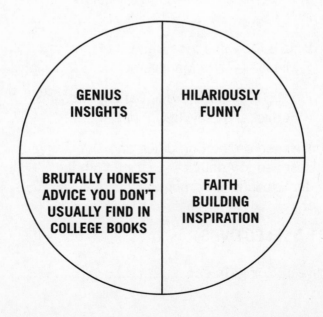

ORIENTATION

AN INTRODUCTION BY THE AUTHORS

A FEW WORDS FROM ROB AND JOE

By the time you graduate from high school, you've learned how things work and you know how to handle every situation. You know where to sit at lunch. You know it's best not to be seen doing homework during lunch. You know that if you're actually going to *do* homework at lunch, there's a table in the corner where some traded food and a few "kind words" will get what's-her-name to do it for you.

But there's more to high school than just lunch period.

You've learned exactly how much time it takes you to study for your trig and American history finals. You're able to make it look like you're working hard in P.E. without breaking a sweat. And you've learned that you need to get a prom or homecoming date at least a month in advance, or else you'll have to go stag.

By the way, you've also learned that *stag* is a four-letter word. Other four-letter words you've learned: *SATs, dumped, pop quiz, just friends,* and *midterm.* Sure, some of those words have more than four letters, but they make you cringe just the same.

Generally speaking, you know who your close friends are — where you fit into the grand scheme of high school things.

But then nature plays a cruel trick: You graduate and suddenly you're not sure of anything.

You've heard about college life and watched a few movies about college. But you don't quite get how it all works. What exactly is a *syllabus*? What does it mean to *rush* a fraternity? What's a credit hour? Will you gain the freshman 15? And should you apply for a credit card now that you can?

Those may be the most obvious questions you're facing. But you'll find yourself in other situations as well. How are you supposed to make new friends? Or find a new church? Are you really supposed to stay up all night writing papers? How does life change with a roommate? What if your roommate is too clean or too messy or stays up all night playing *World of Warcraft,* screaming every time his Level 20 warlock gets attacked? What if your roommate follows you around all the time? What if she doesn't like you?

Those questions mostly manifest themselves in situations that involve going to college, developing your faith, forming new relationships, or getting yourself out of danger. It could be situation 305: What to do when someone breaks up with you because they're "dating Jesus." Or 106: Learning to deal with one of the five types of difficult roommates.

This book is all about those kinds of questions because questions force us to make choices. And the choices you make throughout your college years will define not only your college experience, but also who you are after you graduate.

So choose wisely.

Still, you don't have to choose things on your own. As you live out your college adventure and you encounter a situation or a crisis, you can find the answers here.

See, here's how this book works. Whenever you encounter a problem, you must ...

1. IDENTIFY THE SITUATION

First, we (Joe and Rob — the authors of the book you're currently holding) will describe the types of college situations you might face. If your situations look anything like ours did, then you might have questions such as, "I've been invited to a party, and I'm not sure what to do now." "What if I've started to gain the freshman 15?" Or "I still don't know which college to choose."

This book doesn't have to be read cover to cover at all. You can flip through and open it up as new adventures cross your path. Check out the Contents pages and see which situations you're in and flip to those pages.

However, if you read a situation and it sounds like something you're facing, then the next thing you should do is ...

2. DIAGNOSE THE SYMPTOMS

Every situation has symptoms that show you where things got off track. And those symptoms manifest themselves in different ways, so keep an eye out for them. For instance, if you're struggling with a breakup and you think every sad song on the radio is about you, then you might want to refer to situation 305. Or if you're feeling lonely, then a possible symptom might be that you're looking at other schools' brochures and have considered transferring to one of them at semester (as described in situation 107).

The point is that these symptoms indicate that you have a problem. And if you have a problem, you need to ...

3. FIND THE SOLUTION

Every time you discover a problem, you can use this book to find your way out of a jam. No matter what your college adventure looks like, we've found solutions to many of the problems you'll face. These solutions come from a combination of sources, including —

Personal college experience. The two of us have been to nearly every type of college: State schools, out-of-state schools, private schools, and community colleges. We've also studied in graduate programs, and Joe has a doctorate degree. So we *know* college.

Working with students. Between the two of us, we have more than 15 years of experience working with high school and college students. Therefore, we've worked through most of the problems in this book with actual students.

Talking with college students. While writing this book, we surveyed many college students from all walks of life to find out what their biggest problems were and what tools they needed to overcome them.

Interviews with counselors. We've talked with both high school and college guidance counselors to get their advice on different social and academic pressures that today's students face. Throughout this book we're big advocates of academic counselors, so we wanted to talk with them ourselves.

TV shows and movies. We've watched quite a few TV shows and movies about the college experience. In particular, we know exactly what to do if you're middle-aged and want to go back to college and join a rowdy fraternity, or if you want to go to college in Orange County.

Pastors and leaders. We've talked with pastors and campus group leaders to discover what problems college students are facing and how to resolve them.

As you can see, we leaned on quite a few people in order to create this book. That's something to keep in mind whenever you have to solve a problem of your own — you don't have to do it alone. As *The College Adventure Handbook* will show you, there are friends, professors, parents, advisors, and pastors who are willing to help you work your way through many of the situations you'll encounter.

Some situations can be quickly resolved. So don't hesitate to pull out this book in the middle of a conversation, date, or class period. If you want to be sneaky about it, excuse yourself to the "powder room," "the john," or "the can." When you come back, all of your friends will be amazed at the epiphany you had while you were in the bathroom.

We've divided this book into five different kinds of situations:

- Incoming Situations
- Faith Situations
- Dating Situations
- Dangerous Situations
- Electives

Electives are a hodgepodge of items that we believe are important, but they didn't quite fit in anywhere else. (You should get used to this. Many things in college are a bit of a hodgepodge.) We've also given you the prerequisites — a fancy college term that means "the stuff you should know first" — for each section.

As you read, know that every situation is different because every person is different. For some people, dealing with a breakup will be easy but time management will be impossible — or vice versa. So if you quickly work through one situation — great! And if other situations take more of your time and energy, that's okay, too. You should take the time to find the solution because the bottom line is this: There are lots of tests in college — and not all of them involve No. 2 pencils and Scantron sheets.[1]

College is a place where your character is formed, your career begins, lifelong relationships are formed, and your faith is challenged. (Okay, not just challenged, but attacked outright like a bunch of mean kids poking a puppy behind a dumpster.) However, when your faith and your character are tested … they grow. It may not seem like much fun when an atheist professor calls you out in front of the class because of your beliefs; or you find yourself entrenched in a really unhealthy, fatal-attraction relationship; or you have to stay up all night writing a paper when everyone else is going to the party of the year.

But these are the tests you'll face.

And you *can* pass them.

---

1. Why do teachers always make a big deal about No. 2 pencils? Why don't No. 1 and No. 5 pencils get any love? Was there some conspiracy to make No. 2 pencils the preferred pencil of teachers?

This book is one of the resources that can help you. It shows you practical ways to evaluate problems and make the right decisions to overcome them. And if you can learn how to do these things now, then you'll ultimately have a strong faith, good character, and a great career — not just during college, but also for the rest of your life.

And it can all be yours for just $13.99.[2]

---

2. Of course, you also have to study, pray, do devotionals, make good decisions, network, build friendships, be wise in your relationships — especially those with the opposite sex because they can be really tricky — and get on your professors' good side by giving them Earl Grey tea. We're not sure why, but many professors have a near addiction to some sort of tea. So find out what their favorite tea is. Seriously. Even if it doesn't improve your grade, you've given someone the gift of tea, and that seems like the Christian thing to do.

PART

(INCOMING SITUATIONS) 1

(PREREQUISITE 1: TYPES OF COLLEGE STUDENTS)

BEFORE YOU BEGIN READING "INCOMING SITUATIONS" ...

YOU SHOULD KNOW THAT COLLEGE IS A TIME IN YOUR LIFE WHEN YOU CAN BE WHATEVER YOU WANT.

Scary, isn't it? But there are *some* limiting factors. You won't suddenly be able to dunk a basketball or fit into any pair of jeans you want. But you can control how you present yourself and what you spend your time doing because you get to start a new life.

A lot of new college students look at this unique opportunity as being frightening. They think, *I'm not going to know anyone. I won't have any friends.* Nonsense! Friends are easy to make (see situation 107).

Starting college is a gift — it's one of the few times in life when everyone has a blank slate and can put whatever they want on it. This is exactly why you *should* be thinking, *I can be anyone I want to be.*

You couldn't make a new start in high school because everyone remembers how you threw up on the kickball field in second grade. Or if you moved around a lot while you were growing up, then you were always known as "the new kid." But in college, every freshman on campus is the new kid. So the question you need to ask yourself is, *Who do I want to be?*

To help you answer that, we're now going to describe some different types of college students. You may really identify with one of these types. You may even be a blend of some of them. For the purpose of this book, we've broken it down into four categories: The President, the Romeo or Juliet, the Artist, and the Homework Worm.

THE TYPES

The President   The Romeo   The Artist   The Homework Worm

THE PRESIDENT

Everyone's mom says something like, "Honey, you can be anything you want to be when you grow up. You can *even* be the president of the United States." Most of us probably thought this was just something cheesy our moms said to us because they had to. But the President type of college student believed her mom.

So she relentlessly pursues her dreams. Oftentimes these dreams don't actually entail becoming president of the United States. But it's usually something ambitious — such as becoming a brain surgeon, an astronaut, or a Supreme Court justice. She networks with people all the time. She has a double major. She takes several classes beyond a full course load. She plans to graduate in three years (two and a half if she takes summer classes). Next comes law school. And then it's on to becoming the ruler of the free world.

The Good: If you're the President, you have clear goals and know what you want out of life. You're focused, determined, and ready to do whatever it takes to be successful.

The Bad: College is about more than just networking for the future or getting your resume ready for grad school and a career. Sometimes you can be so focused on the end result that you don't make time for friendships or experiencing the fun of college. You'll regret not doing these things. So study hard and then go with your friends to swim in the fountains by the food court.

THE ROMEO OR JULIET

It's not who you are, it's who you date. This is the governing philosophy of the Romeo or Juliet. They do normal things, such as going to class, but during the lecture they're most likely scanning the room for potential relationships. If this is you, then you probably tried out for your high school's stage production of *The Notebook* because you heard there's a kissing scene halfway through.

There are varying degrees of the Romeo/Juliet. Some fall in love at first sight, believing that every person they lay eyes on is *the One*. If this is you, then you might tell your friend, "He's perfect. He'd make an awesome study partner." But really you're thinking, *He'd make an awesome husband!* And you can easily imagine the two of you taking a honeymoon trip to Maui and making pancakes together on Saturday mornings—all because he said hi to you in chemistry lab.

The Juliet can imagine the ideal husband who will make pancakes every morning.

The Good: Friday nights are never boring.

The Bad: Two words: Relationship drama. When you're Romeo or Juliet, so many of your conversations with friends revolve around questions like these: "Why didn't he call me back?" "Do you think she really likes me?" "Do you think we should be exclusive? Or should we see other people? Should we see other people every other Friday?"

You'll notice that your friends quickly stop caring about your drama. Obviously dating is an important part of college life. (We'll have a lot more about this in the Dating Situations section.) But finding that special someone isn't the *only* part of college life. So don't let yourself become consumed with it.

THE ARTIST

High school students who are really into the arts can often be outcasts. Those who spend all of their time with the theater group or the band frequently find themselves the butt of every band-camp joke and without prom dates.

But in college this gets completely turned around. Suddenly the Artist couldn't be more hip. People think it's edgy that he doesn't wear shoes (or deodorant). In high school you'd either get laughed at or everyone would be unimpressed by your filmmaking efforts. Yet this skill can be totally valued—even worshiped—in college. You can say things like, "I think of my life as one long film," and circles of people will gobble it up. Seriously.

You see, when you're the Artist, your art defines you. You always talk about the new project—song, painting, film—you're working on. And you start using pretentious phrases, such as "the human condition," while everyone oohs and ahhs as though you're Socrates' long lost son.

The Good: If you're the Artist, then you're putting your creativity to good use. And college is the perfect place to develop your passion for music, film, or art. You can find friends, professors, and classes to push you and make you better in your creative endeavors. And if you're talented enough and make the right connections with peers and professors, then it's even possible that your art could pave a way for your career.

The Bad: Sure, the Artist goes to class, but the whole time he's dreaming of black-and-white photography and acoustic guitar riffs for his next song. Much like the Romeo or Juliet, if you're the Artist you might be solely defined by your latest project, which makes you moody and melancholy. You can get crazy when you feel as though your project isn't going the way you want it to or when you face rejection. Perhaps your painting didn't make it into the gallery showing, or your short film wasn't chosen for the festival, or maybe your band didn't get picked to play during the homecoming festivities out on the lawn. You're going to be okay. Rejection is part of putting your art out there, which is why you can't let it be the sole thing that defines you.[1]

THE HOMEWORK WORM

The Homework Worm goes to class and then right back to her dorm-room-cave. If this is you, then your peers look up to you. Or at least they think you're the smartest student in the class. You've actually read the book and done the home-

---

1. If your art is consistently rejected—for instance, if no one listens to or buys CDs of your one-man banjo act—then maybe it's time to find a new creative outlet.

work. And usually you hate group projects because you end up doing most of the work yourself.

But the problem for the Homework Worm is that the classroom is all that matters to her. She knows there's more to college than classes—in theory, anyway. But she can't help but think, *If it won't help my grade, then why bother?*

The Good: If you're the Homework Worm, you'll get good grades on tests and projects that involve only you. And you'll have plenty of time to play video games or watch movies by yourself—if you can keep from studying ahead.

The Bad: It might surprise you to know that after their first year, students like the Homework Worm drop out of college like flies. The emotional stress of not having any relational support isolates a student, which leads to homesickness. And a socially isolated college student is potentially the unhealthiest type of all.

If you find yourself becoming the Homework Worm, *please*—for your own good—read the rest of this book. And pay special attention to situations 107 (coping with loneliness at college) and 301 (getting a smoking hot Christian boyfriend or girlfriend). Nothing deters you from homework like a smoking hot girlfriend or boyfriend. But don't get too deterred, otherwise you'll need to refer to situation 402 (what to do if you're failing a class).

101

I'D RATHER BE A WOLVERINE THAN A BEAVER

CHOOSING A COLLEGE

SITUATION

It's another day in high school, and you're enjoying your lunch of six items from the 99-cent value menu. You look up and see that your friend is wearing a Pepperdine sweatshirt. You ask her, "What's a Pepperdine?"

Your friend says, "It's where I just got accepted!" Then she screams and waves her arms in excitement.

Another friend pipes up, "I'm going to the University of Florida! Yeah!" He stands up and makes chomping alligator arm motions. You think he looks a little foolish, but you're also kind of jealous. At least he has an alligator school to belong to.

You suddenly realize that all of your friends are wearing college T-shirts and sweatshirts. And they have been for weeks. Months even. What's wrong with you? Why aren't you proudly displaying a college bumper sticker on your car? It seems everyone else has chosen a career and knows exactly which college will best prepare them for that job. You don't even know how to go about choosing a college. What are you going to do?

SYMPTOMS

You start watching college football games on TV.
You aren't concerned with the plays as much as you're just waiting for the camera to cut to the students jumping up in down in the stands and giving each other high-fives. You stare at them, and questions race through your head: *Would I fit in there? Could I be friends with these people? What are they talking about between plays—when they're not jumping up and down and giving high-fives? What does everyone do after the game?*

You wonder which mascot best describes you.
You imagine telling all of your friends which mascot best describes you: Rooster—not so much. Gator—maybe. Buckeye—you don't even know what a buckeye is. Wolverine—jackpot! You'd be proud to go to a college whose mascot is named after the indestructible member of the X-Men.

You feel you'd fit in best at a college named after one of the X-Men.

Thinking about going away makes you anxious—thinking about sticking around home makes you depressed.

The thought of getting away from your parents is initially exciting. *I can do whatever I want,* you think. But then you realize you don't know how to do anything: *Do you really have to separate the lights from the darks? What does it mean to file taxes or take out a loan? And how do you fry an egg? How do you scramble one? Shouldn't I at least know how to cook an egg before I go to college?* Not that it matters because you don't even own a frying pan.

You say, "I'm going to take a year off."

Sick of not having an answer when everyone keeps asking, "What are you going to do next year?" you start saying, "I'm taking a year off." It sounds like a good answer. And if you truly want to take a year off to work, save money, or travel the globe—we understand. High school is exhausting.

Note: You need to understand that with every passing year, it gets a lot easier *not* to go back to school. Sometimes "taking a year off" can turn into "I'll start taking classes when I'm 35."

SOLUTION

Step 1: Decide what you're looking for in a college.

The three most important factors of a college are size, cost, and location. Would you be more comfortable on a small, close-knit campus? Or do you want a large school with lots of different clubs, a good football team, and a large campus pond?

Consider your personality as you think through this. For example, if you're extroverted, then at first glance you may think a larger college is the perfect choice for you. The more people you can get to know, the better. But often it's not that simple. Large colleges often lead to large class sizes. You'll have lectures without a lot of one-on-one activity, clubs where it's hard to find your place, and dorms with so many students that it takes awhile to make friends.

And just because you're introverted doesn't mean you shouldn't choose a large college. Large colleges offer classes that are perfect for people who simply want to sit and learn from seasoned experts. They also offer a variety of clubs and groups so you can pinpoint just what you're looking for.

Again, the important detail to figure out is what *are* you looking for? What class sizes will give you the best education? What fields do you want to study—or think you want to study? Is it more important to you that the school has a sweet film program or a chance to make it to the Sweet 16? Do you want to go to college in state or out of state? Is it important for you to travel somewhere new? Are you going to a private school or a state school? If you want to go to a private school, can you afford the tuition?

College is all about putting yourself in the right place for your future, so only you can answer these questions. Decide what you're looking for and then find the college that best matches your needs and your budget.

Step 2: Talk with your parents. (And parents, talk with your student.)

You may have assumptions about what your parents will or won't pay for. You may think they don't care where you go to school. You may think they care too much about where you go. The problem comes when you assume you already know what your parents want or can do to help you (and this is a two-way street). So before you put that college bumper sticker on your car, talk with them.

Things will go a lot more smoothly if you have a unified front. Your parents can help alleviate fears, solve problems, and search out financial aid. Sometimes parents and students feel that if Mom and Dad aren't paying for college, then there's little they can do to help their student. But parents can help look for loans, grants, and scholarships, as well as share experiences about their own college lives. The goal should be for the student and the parent(s) to look at the college experience as a partnership.

College is about students learning to support themselves and make their own decisions. However, as an adult you learn that part of making great decisions is trusting people with good advice.

Like your parents.

The key here is a partnership—students looking to their parents to give good advice, and parents trusting their college-age children to make the right choices.

Step 3: Visit the campus.

This might be the most important step in your decision. It may seem difficult to carve out time to visit a campus. But nothing will answer your questions better than being there. Go midweek. Visit classes. See what sort of social activities happen there. And pay attention to how you feel. You may have thought it was your dream school until you set foot on the campus. Visit a few college campuses so you can compare and contrast.

Most colleges also host weekends designed for prospective freshmen. The school organizes tours and events designed to let you interact with current students as well as other prospective ones. Contact colleges to see if they offer any events like this and register to visit your top schools.

Just about any college campus is going to feel overwhelming at first. Don't let the students breaking out in spontaneous games of Hacky Sack intimidate you. Soon enough you'll feel right at home.

Step 4: Talk to guidance counselors.
Guidance counselors can let you know what you need to be admitted, how to get financial aid, and what majors and career paths the school offers. We interviewed several guidance counselors while writing this book, and both high school and college counselors had the same message, "We're here to help." However, they also said that some students are too scared, confident, lazy, or forgetful to ask for help.

Any college Web site will include some kind of "future student page" where you'll find a wealth of information. But if you don't find what you're looking for there, then don't stop with that page. Contact the school. Many universities have regional representatives who'll be willing to email, talk on the phone, or even meet you in person. Get as much information as possible so you can find the college that's the best fit for you.

102

I'M THE OLDEST KID AT YOUTH GROUP

SAYING GOOD-BYE TO FRIENDS AND FAMILY

SITUATION

You wake up, go downstairs, and pour yourself a bowl of cereal.
You'd planned to eat your breakfast in peace. But when your mom sees you, she starts crying. "Mom? What's the matter?" you ask.

She says, "You're downstairs, you're eating, and you look so cute. It seems like just yesterday that your father and I brought you home from the hospital." Then she launches into a graphic retelling of your birth story. When she finishes, she says, "And now my little baby is all grown up and going away to college, and I'll never come downstairs in the morning and find you eating cereal again."

But it's not just your mom.

Your best friends seem distant, and you no longer feel at home while at church or your job because you're *checking out* and going to college soon.

SYMPTOMS

Your best friends are avoiding you with the following lame excuses:
   a. I have to wash my hair.

   b. I need to walk my dog.

   c. I'm trying out for a role in the new Steven Spielberg movie.

When your best friends fire off each of these excuses all within 24 hours, they're probably pulling away from you because they know you're leaving.

You feel very old at youth group.
It never bothered you before, but now you're irritated by the number of boy band T-shirts and all the candy. It's also annoying that the juniors are constantly pumping their fists and shouting about their upcoming senior year. And you can't believe how small the freshmen look. You were never that small when you were a freshman.

Your girlfriend dumps you.
She simply tells you that long-distance relationships never work. We hate it for you.

SOLUTIONS

Make plans to keep in touch with friends and family.
Every time your mom cries, just tell her you'll call once a week—and text her more often than that. You could even

go so far as to plan the day and the time. "Mom, we'll talk every Thursday at 3." Then stick to it. And you know how your friends communicate best—via texting, Facebook, Web chats, IMing, emails, or phone calls—so contact them. Make sure *you* take the initiative. There's nothing worse than feeling forgotten by a friend.

Leave room for new friendships.
Never grow so attached to your old friendships that you don't leave room for new friends in your life. If you're just starting college, we know you might not believe this yet— we may even sound like your father when we say this. But please listen anyway: The friends you make in college will be some of the best you'll ever have.

So get ready to hit the ground running once you arrive at college. Meet new people. Hang out with new friends. And don't endlessly compare your new friends to your old ones. Appreciate your life back home and your high school friends for who they are, but learn to enjoy your new friends, too.

Don't hold on to long-distance romantic relationships.
Remember the girlfriend who dumped you? At the moment it happens, we know it'll hurt; but having a long-term re-lationship can be detrimental to your first year of college. You won't be out on Friday nights because you'll be talking on the phone and trying to keep your relationship alive. But your lives will be moving in different directions.

Relationships change, and that's okay.

Your relationships with your parents and friends will undergo some changes throughout your adult life. They'll change when you go to college, when (if) you get married, and when (if) you have kids. In college, your friends will be some of the most important people in your life, and your parents can now step back and admire—from afar—your accomplishments and the person you're becoming.

Don't get too relaxed—Mom and Dad will still bring down the thunder from on high if you do something irresponsible like forget to go to class for half a semester and fail a course.

Say good-bye well.

Saying good-bye is a part of life. So there are two options: (1) Slink off to college without saying good-bye to your closest friends or (2) celebrate! Plan a party or go on a camping trip with your high school friends. You could even take a road trip to Six Flags or Disney World.

Sometimes we get so nervous and excited about what's next that we forget to celebrate what we've accomplished and the friendships we've made. Don't let that happen. Celebrate with your friends. Then get ready to pack up and head off to school.

103

SHOULD I CALL YOU "DR. PROFESSOR" OR JUST "PROFESSOR"?

THE DIFFERENCES BETWEEN HIGH SCHOOL AND COLLEGE

SITUATION

You're feeling proud of yourself.
You've chosen a college, packed up your things, and said good-bye to your family and friends. You've moved out of your home and gotten a roommate. You've registered for classes, and your first one starts tomorrow.

But as Sunday night ticks down and Monday morning nears, you realize you have no idea what to expect. You're not sure what college life is really like. You're not sure how different your classes, classmates, and teachers will be from high school. You're not sure what to do after class or before class. What's the difference between high school and college teachers?

Your new roommate informs you they're not called "teachers" anymore. They're "professors." Call a college professor "Mr. Teacher" and you can expect that the rest of the semester in his class won't go smoothly.

If you've fallen prey to any of the symptoms, you may have a problem. But if you're currently suffering from these symptoms, fret not. We have just the solutions to help you out.

SYMPTOMS

You stayed up all night because no one told you to go to bed.

As you waved good-bye to Mom and Dad during orientation weekend, you realized there's so much to do. There's an all-night Texas hold 'em tourney going on three dorm rooms down. A group of girls invited everyone to a pedicure party in the next dorm. And you just discovered a McDonald's that starts serving breakfast at 4 a.m. In your first 72 hours of college, you can't remember the last time you slept.

You forget to go to class because the bell didn't ring.

During lunch you start joking around with your new friends and completely lose track of time. When you finally look at the clock, you realize class is almost over. How were you supposed to know? In high school there were security guards walking around with walkie-talkies and guard dogs to make sure you didn't skip class. But here, no one even hints that you need to get to class.

You don't turn in a paper—and no one notices.

As class begins, everyone takes their freshly completed papers to the front of the room. You sit at your desk and cringe, just waiting for the professor to say, "Excuse me. Where's your paper?" But he never does.

Makeup exam is a foreign term to your professors.
You missed a test. So you go to your professor and tell her you need to take a makeup test. She looks at you like she has no idea what you're talking about—because she doesn't. Makeup tests don't happen in college unless you've either arranged for one ahead of time (even then, you're often told no) or had a really good excuse.

And in college you can't just make up excuses. If you say you were sick, then you'd better have a note from the doctor. (That note should probably say you were having some sort of major surgery.) If you say your grandmother passed away, then you might need to show your professor the obituary.

THINGS NO LONGER COOL IN COLLEGE

▶ Mom driving you to school so you don't have to take the bus.

▶ Eating out every day.

▶ Not doing your homework.

▶ Dad helping you pay for taking a girl out.

▶ Dating high schoolers.

SOLUTION

Pace yourself.

In high school there were certain boundaries in place to keep you safe. But just because you're unrestrained now, that doesn't mean you should try and experience everything. Yet this is a common problem for some students who come from a strong Christian background.

If that's you, then you may feel as though you were pretty sheltered at home. But honestly, it's okay to be sheltered from some things. So thank Mom or Dad for their protection and resist the urge to try everything the moment you step on campus. Otherwise, you may eventually regret something you try on a whim.

You're going to spend at least four years in college. You don't have to expose yourself to everything during the first week.

With great power comes great responsibility.

It's like Uncle Ben told his nephew Peter Parker: "With great power comes great responsibility." This may be the first time you've ever had this level of responsibility. During high school you may not have been completely free to make your own decisions. Perhaps there were parents, teachers, youth pastors, and big sisters telling you when you were nearing trouble.

Now that you're away from home and those people who've always provided so much structure, you may not even realize you're near the edge—until you fall off. This means you have to pay attention and be responsible. You have to understand that if you eat or drink too much, you'll get sick. If you skip class and don't turn in papers, you'll fail. There's no more handholding. No one is going to make you do anything.

But there's still plenty of help and support out there. You can get help with writing your papers. You can find tutors to explain what that crazy psychology lecture was all about. You have the power of freedom and the responsibly to succeed.

College is a beautiful and scary thing, isn't it?

Read all of your syllabi—create a calendar.
If you're new to college, you may not know that all of your professors will conspire against you to make your academic life unbearable. During every semester there will be weeks when things pile up. You'll have two quizzes, a midterm, and a 10-page paper all on the same day.

Ask any college student—this happens.

The best way to guard against this eventuality is to anticipate it. During every first class, you'll receive a syllabus. Once you have all of your syllabi, read through them and find the weeks where projects and assignments appear to stack on top of each other.[2] Plan to turn in papers and study for those tests early. This is how those overly ambitious President students master their difficult schedules.

---

2. Yes, *syllabi* is the plural of *syllabus*. Technically, you can also call them "syllabuses," but doing so could be an indication to all of your professors and friends that you haven't quite grasped the differences between high school and college. So we'd recommend saying *syllabi*—unless you're just a rebel.

104

I THOUGHT *STREAKING* INVOLVED WINDEX

THE TRANSITION FROM HOME SCHOOL TO COLLEGE

SITUATION

On your day first of school, you realize there are about 50,000 more people at your college than there were at your home school. This is a little intimidating.

Instead of history lessons in the kitchen with your mother, there's a lecture hall filled with 300 other people. And you can no longer go to class in your pajamas. (Okay, that's not entirely true. Some college students go to class in their pajamas. Just make sure you're wearing pajamas that you'd be comfortable having your friends and professors see.)

You were used to working at your own pace, but now you have to wait for the professor to cover new material before you can blaze ahead. Now you have to work on projects with other students. One person in your group never comes to class, and another texts her friends the whole time you're supposed to be working on the project.

These new adjustments are hard, and you can't help but hate college. It's so inefficient. So impersonal. And to make things worse, you don't really know how to fit in. So far college is a pretty major letdown. And you're going to be here for a while—Christmas break is still four months away.

SYMPTOMS

No one is impressed that you were the prom queen of the home school association's dance.
In fact no one really cares about your high school experiences at all. Your roommates swap stories about homecoming games and prom, and they don't seem interested in that field trip/family vacation you took to D.C. last summer. You feel left out of a lot of conversations. The reality is that their high school experiences were different than yours, and it's left you feeling isolated and insecure.

You have to wait until the end of the semester to take the final.
Throughout your school career, you always moved at your own pace. Whenever you'd mastered a subject, you'd take the test and move on to the next thing. But now some of your classes are moving too quickly while others are moving too slowly. In Spanish 101, for instance, the class is still learning how to say, "Where is the bathroom?" and you just have to sit and mutter "¿Dónde está el baño?" with the rest of the class. You think, *I've known where the bathroom is since eighth grade*. And if that weren't bad enough, el profesor says you have to wait until the end of the semester to take the final.

You think the drink is called "jungle juice" because you're going to a *Lion King* theme party.

But when you arrive, you soon realize there's nothing *Lion King* themed at all. There is stuff called "jungle juice," however. It's in a plastic kiddie pool, and there's so much alcohol in it that it smells like nail polish remover.

This new terminology isn't the only college slang that surprises you. In your first week alone, you learned terms like *frat* and *commons*. And when you were invited to go *streaking*, you brought a bottle of window cleaner and shouted, "All right! Let's get our streak on!"

Just because the drink is called "jungle juice" doesn't mean you're going to a Lion King theme party.

SOLUTION

If you haven't started college yet, get involved.
Make sure you're finding groups to connect with. The reality is that home school communities can offer sporting co-ops, large social events, dances, and more. The more home school events you get involved with, the easier the transition to college will be. Home-schooled high school students can also enroll in community college to get some general education classes out of the way—which is also a good way to get used to a college classroom. (Just make sure the credits transfer to your college of choice.)

You don't have to expose yourself to everything.
We just mentioned this in situation 103, but it's worth repeating. Just because you're away from home doesn't mean you should go to your first alcohol party and drink so much that you stand on top of the refrigerator and declare yourself the Queen of Scotland. There are many new experiences to be found in college, and you don't need to find the most outrageous ones.

Embrace home school pride.
One of the great things about home school was all the things you got to experience. You may have been able to travel more, learn interesting subjects, and grow closer to your family. Don't back away from that. Be proud of your home school background. So you didn't get to sit through a study hall or deal with crowded hallways—so what? Who cares if you were never stuffed inside a locker? Your experiences

made you who you are today. Don't be arrogant, but you *can* embrace home school pride.

A month from now, high school won't matter.
In the first month of college, a lot of your conversations will revolve around where you come from and your past high school experiences. But after that, you'll find your own friends and start having new experiences and making new memories. Where you came from won't seem as important. Instead, the type of person and friend you are will be what matters the most.

THE FIRST REAL DECISION YOU'LL EVER HAVE TO MAKE

DECLARING A MAJOR

SITUATION

It's freshmen orientation—time to pick out the first semester's schedule.

You're looking at the course catalogue online, and you realize it has more pages than an online novel. In high school you had one choice for an elective: Band or choir. Now there are all of these classes. How do you know what to take? They all seem important for your future success.

Now you're waiting in line at campus registration, and the kid next to you is arrogantly going on and on about how he's going to double-major in engineering and math to assure his future at NASA as the first person to land on Mars. If you weren't a Christian, you'd choke this little space-nerd's neck. Why should he know the exact plan for his life when you're struggling to make lunch plans?

This section is all about picking a major so you can graduate in four years. Graduating on time and with a major (even a minor!) is kind of the goal of college. This chapter will give you the big picture perspective and help you avoid dillydallying your way to a sixth—or even a seventh—year.

SYMPTOMS

You've already changed your major six times before the first day of class.

You're the kind of person who changes hobbies every other week. One day you're sewing your own dress; the next day the dress is in the trash and you're learning to play the guitar while writing a song about how no one understands you. People tell you all the time to stick with something, but you love the thrill of doing something new.

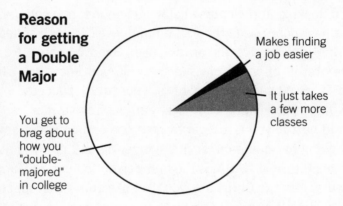

Reason for getting a Double Major

Makes finding a job easier

It just takes a few more classes

You get to brag about how you "double-majored" in college

You're over-spiritualizing every "sign" for your life's direction.

A car passes by. Its license plate has the letters R and D. You instantly ask, *Could these letters be backward? Does God want me to see the letters DR? Does this mean God wants me to be a premed student?*

The fact is that you have yet to make any decision pertaining to the goal of graduating because you're waiting for

God's clear, audible, and unmistakable direction. There-fore, instead of pushing forward, you're proudly sitting there without any sense of direction so as not to make the wrong move with your life.

You imagine yourself as an astronaut-firefighter who also fights crime.

You can't even choose a candy bar at a convenience store. Decisions scare you because you don't want to be limited and labeled. And when you start thinking about your ca-reer, you think, *Maybe I should be an astronaut ... or a crime fighter. Maybe I could fight crime in space.*

If you can't decide on a major, you might start imagining yourself
as a crime fighting astronaut firefighter.

SOLUTION

Set goals and relax.

Your life's destiny doesn't depend on whether you take English 101 this semester or next. Many of the college experts we talked with said that most college students don't pick their majors until their *junior year*. Even more impressive are the statistics that show that a large majority of college graduates land jobs in fields that aren't even related to their majors.

You should relax and be encouraged that you're getting a degree. It can open doors into your future and the plans God has for you. Just keep in mind the goal of graduating. Then take the classes and do the schoolwork required to achieve that goal.

Take classes in majors that interest you.

If you're unsure about choosing a major, take a few classes to get an idea. Take a film production class if you think you'd like to learn to make movies, a psychology class if you want to go into counseling, or a science class if you want to do scientific stuff. (Sorry, we'd give a more specific example if we really understood what scientists do. But we're sure it's very important.)

The point is if you have interests but aren't sure you're ready to commit to a major, then just explore some classes to see what's out there.

Don't wait for the audible voice of God before choosing an elective.

God speaks to us in many ways, and you should definitely pray and ask God to guide your decisions. But you should also listen to common sense, pastors, teachers, and family. Colleges are full of Christians who are just waiting around for some huge calling from God — while God may be whispering for them to pick a direction and start moving toward something they know is good.

Meet with your academic advisor. Then meet with her again.

Every college student has an academic advisor. Students can usually find out who their advisor is before they arrive on campus. Get on a first name basis with yours. An advisor can help you find your strengths and narrow down a major. Most importantly, an advisor can set up your class schedule to help you graduate quicker and without wasting time in classes you don't really need.

INSIDER TIPS FOR GRADUATING IN FOUR YEARS

▶ **Pick classes that fulfill general education requirements.**

Pepper your schedule with electives that you're interested in majoring in. For example, if you're thinking about becoming an

English major, consider taking a creative writing class because it will count toward your major. And this is true of most majors—business classes will relate to business majors, biology classes to biology majors, and so on.

However, if you're not sure about your major, don't go crazy with electives during your first two years. If you ever change your major, those classes may not apply to your new major or minor. Focus instead on the general classes that all majors are required to take.

▶ **Register early.**
Even before you buy your bedsheets and show up on campus, you should begin planning your semester of classes. Once you have a student ID, you can beat the rush of registration to get into the classes you need and want.

▶ **Just register for the class!**
If in doubt, register for the course you think you need or want. There are rarely any penalties for dropping a class before the first day. *It's better to be registered for a class and find out you don't need it than to need a class and find out it's already full.*

▶ **Ask for favors from your advisors.**
Your advisors may seem like friendly people who are smiley and helpful. But when it's time to get tough, they can pull strings like the Mafia. Have you ever wondered about all of those students who signed up for a class only to drop it the week after it began? Maybe those students just "disappeared," if you know what we mean. . . .

FIVE DIFFICULT ROOMMATES
LEARNING TO GET ALONG WITH THOSE YOU LIVE WITH

SITUATION

You have a big midterm tomorrow morning.
You've studied and prepared in every way you know how, and now you need to head back to the dorm room to sleep. But the thought of going to your room makes you anxious, nervous, frightened, sick, annoyed, or maybe all of the above.

Why? Because your roommate is there.

For the last few weeks, you've been spending lots of time in coffee shops, the bookstore, the campus dining area, and the grocery store. Eventually you just crash in a friend's room, and your room becomes a place where you store your stuff. Now you've started losing sleep, and you're feeling irritable. You want to stab your roommate with a No. 2 pencil just to see what happens.

Is this what Jesus would do?

No.

Do you care?

No.

Learning to live with a roommate is one of the unique challenges of college life. Sometimes a roommate is someone you knew before college; other times it's someone you've never met. To help you navigate the murky room-mate waters, we've listed five types and some ways to deal with the situation.

SYMPTOMS (TYPES)

The 5 different roomates.

The Slob

The Slob will decorate the dorm room with undergarments and half-full bowls of Ramen noodles. The Slob can go an entire semester without doing laundry. The Slob has no boundaries, and his clothing and toiletries may creep onto your bed, sink, and laundry basket. The Slob can also eat your oatmeal cream pies. The Slob will borrow your clothes, your shampoo, your laptop, and your books without asking. The Slob will say, "You can borrow my stuff, too," but this seems a little unfair because the Slob's T-shirts smell like cottage cheese and Crunch Berries cereal.

The Mom

You won't have to worry about a clean place if you live with the Mom. She'll make sure things are spotless.[3] She'll want every item of clothing starched, ironed, and hung neatly in its place. If she's displeased, sometimes she'll let you know directly, or maybe she'll just sigh a lot or make passive-aggressive comments like, "It sure seems like a while since it's been spic-and-span around here, don't you think?"

But things go beyond cleanliness for the Mom. If you're watching TV for too long, she'll say, "Don't you have a mid-term next week?" If you're out too late, she'll say, "Don't you have to be up early tomorrow?" When she says things like this, you'll just stare at her and feel very, very bad for her unborn children.

The Shadow

Luckily, the Shadow is the most agreeable of the five room-mates. In fact, he'll agree with just about anything you have to say. And he'll be around. All. The. Time. He'll ask, "Where are we going tonight?" even though you never made plans. If you're going on a date, the Shadow will say, "We can double date!" Shadows will show up randomly at

---

3. The Mom doesn't have to be female—guys can be just as motherly when it comes to control-freak issues.

meals, sporting events, and movies. He may even match his class schedule with yours—just to make sure you get more "quality time" together.

When you say, "I'm going to the library to study," the Shadow will say, "I need to hit the books myself." When you say, "I really need some alone time," the Shadow will say, "I agree. Let's hang out—just the two of us tonight."

The Gamer

The Gamer, on the other hand, will leave you alone. He'll turn on the Xbox Live and disappear for days at a time.[4] He may go to class; but as soon as he gets back, he'll flip on the gaming console. Gamers seem to be at their prime around 2 a.m. when they're almost zombie-like, sucked in by the neon-blue glow of the monitor.

The Plus One

You think it's great that your roommate has a girlfriend. Really you do. It's just that she hangs around so much that you're starting to feel like a third wheel. It's kind of like your roommate and his girlfriend are playing house, and you're just crashing the party.

She watches TV with you guys. She has some of her clothes stored in his closest. In fact, she's around so much that you're not sure she really has her own room. You like the fact that she brought a vanilla candle over to make your room smell like sugar cookies. But you hate that you've

---

4. It doesn't have to be an Xbox or even a video game. Some Gamers disappear with books, movies, or computer sites.

now seen every romantic comedy at the video store because that's all she ever wants to watch.

SOLUTION

Confront your roommate.
Living with a roommate involves seeing someone all the time. You can't let things fester. Have a conversation about the things that are bothering you. Do it nicely. Maybe buy your roommate a cup of coffee and say, "Is there anything we can do to help keep the place a little cleaner?" *or* "Do we have to keep the place so clean?"

If the TV is on when you have a final to study for, ask your roommate if she can watch it quietly. If he's borrowing your towels and leaving them in wet piles on the floor, tell your roommate that's kind of annoying. If you want to borrow her shirt, ask her. If it's a brand-new shirt, let her wear it for a while first.

Don't expect your roommate to read your mind. Roommates don't have superpowers. They can't understand what every facial expression, sigh, or slamming of the door is supposed to mean. Talk to your roommate. Use words and sentences to express your feelings.

Create social boundaries.
Roommates can be some of the best friends you'll ever have, so try to foster that friendship. If your roommate is disappearing on the computer all the time, invite him to

come out with you and your friends. Ask your roommate about his life, his interests, his hopes, dreams, and favorite TV shows.

But understand that college is a turbulent place with lots of changes. A heavy class load, a new relationship, a part-time job, or more responsibility can weigh heavily on a roommate. Give him space to process it all. If you feel like you're smothering your roommate, give him space. If your roommate is smothering you, tell him, "We can hang out on Thursday, but on Wednesday I can't do anything."

Understand that *you* are one of the five difficult roommates.
This may shock you. Or you may already know this. But you have some of the tendencies of one of the five roommates. You may be a little too messy, or motherly, or smothering, or lost in your computer, or too busy for a roommate you were once close to. We're not saying you're an extreme case, but there's at least a little part of one of these five types in you. Decide which one you are, and work on ways to improve.

Talk to your Resident Advisor.
Your Resident Advisor (RA) is one of the people who's paid to make sure things go well in your dorm. If you really feel as though you're at an impasse with your roommate, bring in an RA as a mediator. Say something like, "I really would like to get along with my roommate, but there's been a pair of her gym socks sitting in a bowl of noodles for the last

two weeks, and I just can't live like this. What should we do?"

Change rooms at the end of the semester.

If all else fails, then you do have the right to transfer rooms at the semester break.

Learn to get along with your difficult roommate—it will help you later in life.

If you change rooms, the good news is that you'll have a new roommate. The bad news is that your new roommate will probably be a different type of one of the five difficult roommates. This is just how it goes.

Sharing space with someone is something you're going to have to get used to. If you grew up as an only child—or with your own bedroom for your whole life—this may be a difficult challenge for you.

But it's part of college.

And someday you may get married, and you'll have to share nearly everything: Cars, food, checking accounts, a bed, the TV—everything except your wardrobe. This may sound romantic. Or horrifying. Either way, it's the truth. Learning to work out things with a roommate early on will help you in your eventual marriage. Even if you never want to get married, you may not be able to afford a place of your own for a while, so you're still going to have to learn to get along with others.

Solve problems. Build friendships. You may even learn to really like your roommates.

LEFT BEHIND ON FRIDAY NIGHT?

COPING WITH LONELINESS AT COLLEGE

SITUATION

Friday night in the college dorms ... 11 p.m.
Your dorm is a ghost town. It's like the rapture happened. Only in this rapture, it was just the cool, popular, and romantically involved who got taken. You imagine what everyone else is doing right now. You picture a cute couple strolling on the beach and gazing into each other's eyes while they eat soft serve ice cream. You imagine a party that every single person at your college is at—except you.

You're alone. You're lying on the bed in your dorm room feeling hopeless, sad, and lonely. Yet you keep telling yourself, *Be strong ... be strong.* You cried yourself to sleep last night, but tonight is different. Tonight you're going to memorize the lyrics to "With or Without You" by U2 instead of "Tears in Heaven" by Eric Clapton.

SYMPTOMS

You keep mistaking complete strangers for your friends.
You pass by strangers thinking they're someone you know from high school, but right before you smile and wave—you realize it's not them. The fact is, you miss your friends.

You miss drag racing with the shopping carts through the sporting goods section of Wal-Mart. You start to wonder if you'll ever have friends who are that close again.

The Good Old Days

You can't make new friends.
You meet a group of nice people in your dorm. You've had a good conversation and plan to hang out that night, only to find out they like dressing up as different Harry Potter

characters. Or maybe they reenact *High School Musical*. Or they invite you to join them in a round of strip Monopoly.

Why can't you find some normal people you fit in with? Why can't you find some real friends? Everyone else seems to have somewhere to fit in. *Is it possible that* I'm *the weird one?* you think. *Is it possible that I don't fit in here?*

The grass looks greener in the other school's brochure.
You're already feeling like this whole college-away-from-home thing is a big mistake. You feel as though you made the decision too quickly. Now you're sitting alone in your dorm room getting all teary-eyed while looking through that other university's brochure depicting blond girls wearing wire-rimmed glasses and cute boys sitting in the grass studying poetry. You start looking into what it would take to transfer there next semester.

SOLUTION

Loneliness and feeling out of place may, in fact, be the number one problem that beginning college students face. Normally our solutions have a few things you can do to solve the problem. But because loneliness is such an epidemic—which means you're not alone—we've listed nine (count them, *nine*) solutions.

Play the orientation games.
You may want to skip a gathering where a bunch of college freshmen do the chicken dance while trying to find a partner. Don't. Go to these silly events. Get yourself out there.

You'll be glad you did—trust us. Jump into every opportunity with both feet. This is the quickest way to find a new community and group of friends. Don't think you're too cool to go to the ice cream bash, ultimate Frisbee tournament, and the midnight showing of *Star Wars* on the campus lawn. Because—let's face it—you're not that cool. Neither is anyone else. Have fun, get involved.

Bring your "A" game to the chicken dance.

Discover a world outside of Facebook.

The great thing about email, chat rooms, and social networking sites is they let you keep in touch with old friends and find new ones. Or at least it's great in moderation. But if you're spending all of your time with *computer friends*—as witty and funny and cool as they might be—it's not necessarily going to help you get connected at college. If you're feeling isolated, turn off your computer, go outside, and talk to someone who's actually standing in front of you.

Live on campus.
Your off-campus apartment might make you feel more grown-up or more *on your own*. But there's a reason it's called "on your own." Because that's exactly what you are. You may not want to live in dorm rooms where you have to share a room, endure noise, and go into shower stalls that breed new types of fungus. But this is what college life is about. In the dorms it's far easier to get connected, get to know people, and be a part of the campus. So live in the dorms—at least for the first year.

Leave your door open.
If you're going to stay in your room, leave your door open. You'll be amazed at the types of people you can meet just by not shutting your door. Shutting your door says you *want* to be alone.

Do your homework in public.
Be around people if you're feeling lonely. Do your homework at the library, the campus coffee shop, or out on the lawn—even if you don't know anyone there. Get out of your dorm so you're around other students.

Join the club.
The great thing about clubs and groups is they're designed to help you do things and meet people with similar interests. At the student activities center (or whatever it's called on your campus), there are lists of clubs. Many of these will advertise themselves with booths, cookies, candy, T-shirts, and other bribes.

Talk to at least one person in every one of your classes.
Breaking the ice is always easier at the beginning of your class. Chances are you're sitting next to another freshman who's just as nervous and feels as out of place as you do. Who knows? They could be your new BFF or BFFL or BFANF. You'll never know unless you take a chance and meet them.

Go to church.
Church is designed to be a place where people get together, worship, and support each other in life. It's often a sure-fire place to find community as well. (For more on finding a church, go to situation 204.)

Give it time.
The first month or so of college is filled with huge highs and deep lows. At one moment you're on a rollercoaster high because a cute boy just said, "How are you doing?" And in the next moment you realize the boy said hi because static cling hiked up your skirt. This is normal. (Not the skirt part. That's kind of weird—please make sure your skirt isn't hiked up. But the part about highs and lows is

completely normal.) Think about it this way: If you end up looking at other schools' brochures and transferring somewhere, you'll have to go through this first-month phase all over again.

PART 2

$\left(\begin{array}{c}\text{FAITH}\\\text{SITUATIONS}\end{array}\right)$

(PREREQUISITE 2: TYPES OF CHRISTIANS IN COLLEGE)

BEFORE YOU BEGIN READING "FAITH SITUATIONS" ...

YOU SHOULD KNOW THERE ARE MANY STATISTICS THAT SAY YOU'RE LIKELY TO LOSE YOUR FAITH IN COLLEGE.

Some say that as many as 89 percent of graduating high school seniors won't remain Christians by the time they finish a four-year school.

We're not interested in the math of it. We don't know what the odds are for you—or for anyone. Are you more likely to stay a Christian if you like country music or hip-hop? Are you more likely to stay a Christian depending on the time of year you were born? In other words, are summer babies more godly than babies born during the cold winter months—or vice versa? It's tough to say for sure.

What we do know is that college is a time when your faith will be tested—more like flat-out assaulted. Picture a fifth grade bully with an M-80 and a row of porcelain toilets. Or a magnifying glass aimed at an ant colony on a 100-degree day. You get the idea.

If you're going to survive college with your faith intact, then there are a few things you must understand about having faith in college:

YOUR PARENTS AREN'T AROUND ALL THE TIME (AND NEITHER IS YOUR YOUTH PASTOR).

In high school you had a system in place. You knew what to believe — partly because you adopted what your parents believe. And their beliefs are a part of your life just like eating dinner as a family and doing chores on Saturday. Then all of a sudden your mom isn't around to ask you things like, "Have you read your Bible?" or "What did you learn at youth group?"

Just because your mom isn't asking doesn't mean you should skip church altogether. Our parents give us guiding principles and ideas by which to live our lives. But when they're gone, will you continue to believe? Your dad is no longer waking you up on Sunday mornings to go to church. Your youth pastor isn't challenging you every week to pray and read your Bible. Now *you* have to decide whether or not to do these things.

IT'S OKAY TO ASK QUESTIONS.

College is a time when your view of the world should expand. When you get to college, you don't expect to have a complete understanding of astrophysics and English composition. However, if you've grown up in a church, you may feel as though you should already understand everything about God.

When there are areas of your faith that you don't understand, you can get frustrated, annoyed, or even cynical about your belief in God. But the truth is that you don't know it all.

And you don't have to. Ask questions.

IT'S IMPORTANT TO FIND CHRISTIAN FRIENDS.

Instead of sitting back with your arms crossed, grumbling, and letting cynicism set in, find a group of Christian friends. (We'll talk about finding a church or campus ministry a little later.) We're not saying that *all* of your friends should be Christians. In fact, you should be meeting lots of different types of people in college. But there should be people with whom you can be honest and talk about those areas where you're struggling and areas of doubt in your life. In other words, you must be transparent.

Finally, it may help you to know what type of Christian you are. We've described four different types, and you may be a combination of them. Or maybe you're one type but wish you were a different one. Either way, it's good to know where you — and others — fit on this list of types so you know how to navigate faith situations in college.

THE TYPES

The Reverend   The Backslider   The Monk   The Skeptic

THE REVEREND

The easiest way to know if you're the Reverend is if your nonbelieving friends actually refer to you as the "Reverend." Other typical nicknames include "Goody Two-Shoes," "Brainwasher," or the "Religious Girl."

If you're the Reverend, then you probably love going places and handing out invitations to Christian campus events. Oftentimes the Reverend will get into well-meaning debates with people over religious matters, only to have her face turn red as she screams, "Every single one of you needs to accept Jesus, or you'll all be going to hell!" When everyone then stares at her, she'll awkwardly say, "And have a nice day."

The Good: Of all the types of college Christians, the Reverend has the most potential to make it through college with her faith intact because she's not afraid to stand out and be different.

The Bad: At times the Reverend may try so hard to stand out that she isolates herself or alienates everyone around her. Christ called us to be "salt of the earth" (Matthew 5:13 — more on this in situation 201). That means we have to learn to blend in, make friends, and *show* the love of Christ — not just talk about it.

THE BACKSLIDER

College is filled with Christians who come to college with high hopes of going to church, kissing dating good-bye, and listening only to Christian music. The sad reality is that in a few months, many of these same Christians will be sucking on the business end of a beer bong while everyone chants, "Chug! Chug! Chug!"

Other Backsliders live good college lives, but they left their Bibles at home and haven't been to church since arriving on campus. They can't remember the last time they prayed to God — except for a quick prayer before a test they didn't study for.

The Good: The Backslider has a knack for making friends and fitting in. He can fit into any group so well that many times members of that group will think he's the founder.

The Bad: Unlike the Monk, the Backslider's Christian friends are often in the distance. If all your friends are into parties, drinking, and hook-ups (usually in that order), it's just a matter of time until you lower your own standards. The

Backslider needs to get some good friends — no matter how painful it may be to say good-bye to the bad friends.

THE MONK

The Monk lives at church — sometimes literally, due to an internship or round-the-clock volunteering and the abundance of free coffee at church meetings. The Monk avoids any kind of social interaction that isn't with a fellow believer or couldn't in some way be defined as a Bible study, a prayer meeting, fellowship, or witnessing. If the Monk gets invited to see a movie, you can be sure he'll (a) decline, (b) walk out when he hears a swear word, or (c) discuss the sinfulness of the secular world as soon as the end credits roll.

The Good: The Monk avoids a lot of temptation by retreating into his Christian bubble. And he's often part of a good community and well connected to some good causes and events at church or with church friends.

The Bad: He's missing out on lots of opportunities, friendships, and places by staying within the church walls. And that's not all he's missing out on. Jesus told us we should be *a light on a stand, not a light that's hidden* (Matthew 5:14–16). Seems pretty clear. Get out there!

THE SKEPTIC

Your becoming this kind of Christian is exactly what your Bible-believing parents fear the most. One day you're reading your Bible and shouting "Amen!" during church. The next day you're reading a blog about aliens and — *wham!* — you now have a collection of New Age crystals that you use to communicate with the mother planet, and you no longer believe in God. At least that's how it happens in your parents' minds.

The truth isn't that simple. Nothing happens to you overnight. You've had doubts about Christianity for a long time. And it's not that you've given up on faith. You're just not sure you're finished exploring, and you don't want to be forced into anything.

The Good: You've seen the data we mentioned earlier. Our youth pastors used it to scare us all: The majority of Christians will lose their faith when they go to college. Unfortunately, the statistics are real. However, if you begin losing your faith in college, there's a pretty good chance you never actually made your faith *your own*. Did you go to church just because your parents bribed you with allowance money? Did you respond to an altar call to get the attention of a cute girl? Get back to the basics and know why you believe what you believe.

The Bad: Isn't it obvious? This kind of Christian might not be a Christian at all. College is a time of testing your faith, but it's important to return to reason. Return to what you know is true. It's really not that cool to be the renegade who always has something negative to say.

IS ANYONE ELSE STUPID ENOUGH TO BELIEVE IN JESUS?

DEALING WITH THE CHALLENGES OF FEELING ISOLATED FOR YOUR FAITH

SITUATION

Philosophy seems like your sort of elective—the type of class where you can get away with anything. For instance, you can choose not to turn in your homework and then when your professor asks, "Where's your homework?" you can reply, "*Life* is homework." Your answer will sound so deep that you'll probably get an A on the spot.

This is how you picture philosophy class.

The reality is pretty different. People toss around words like *metaphysical* and *existential.* And then during one of the first major philosophical debates of the course, religion comes up. Soon afterward the topic of politics and Christianity comes up. That's when a girl in the front row shouts, "Why would anyone ever think that? Is anyone stupid enough to believe in Jesus?"

You think, *I'm stupid enough to believe in Jesus.* But you realize that's not quite how you want to answer the question. So you quietly sit at your desk and wonder if anyone else has faith like you do.

SYMPTOMS

You think apologetics involves apologizing.

You find yourself apologizing for being a Christian.[1] You make light of your beliefs and minimize everything in the Bible whenever you're talking with non-Christian friends. If they ask you about hell, you just apologize and say how you wish God would get everyone out of hell and give them all puppies.

This isn't apologetics.

---

1. "Apologetics" means giving a reason for your faith. It has nothing to do with apologizing.

When asked about your faith, you change the subject to your friend's cat named Faith.

Do you look for the closest exit and disappear when friends start a conversation about religion? This symptom is different than apologizing for your faith. It just plain ignores it or changes the subject away from anything spiritual.

You just cussed at an atheist.

Some superhero Christians feel as though it's their job to engage every religious debate ever waged. If you find yourself yelling theology at random strangers while leaving coffee shops, you might be overdoing it a tad. This symptom is the opposite of apologizing or ignoring.

SOLUTION

Be salt.

We're called to be the salt of the earth. Have you ever thought about salt? It's used as a seasoning. A small order of French fries covered in a half-pound of salt would be disgusting. Just a pinch will do.

In the same way, you should season your conversations with Christ. For example, there are going to be times in your life when friends will want to know why you're so different, and these moments will be great opportunities for you to tell them about your faith. However, these same friends probably won't want to hear about your faith when they're bragging about cheating on a midterm. Choose your moments wisely.

Put them on the defense.
Believe it or not, you don't have to retreat with a white flag in hand whenever a non-Christian asks about your faith. Try to find out—in a respectful way—where she's placing her faith. Ask pointed questions that challenge the foundation of what she believes. The conversation will inevitably get sidetracked to legalizing marijuana, the big bang theory, polygamy, and other such random topics. When this happens try to bring her back to what's really at the core of her spiritual beliefs and ask what's holding her back from a belief in Jesus.

Consider the debate won if the person has seen the love of Christ and some amount of truth has been spoken.
The Bible says the truth of the gospel is foolishness to nonbelievers.[2] For a fellow college student or professor to understand and experience the saving grace of Jesus, God must first be at work in that person's heart. You don't have to feel like a failure if it seems as though you've lost the debate with a non-Christian. Just engage in a conversation and respectfully explain why you've placed your trust in Christ.

Be strong.
Christians in college can get pretty beat up by people of other faiths—or no faith—who love to criticize what we believe. It's fashionable these days to be searching for your faith. But once someone claims she's found it, she

---

2. 1 Corinthians 2:14

can be ridiculed. People might tell you something like, "You're supposed to be searching for faith—not *deciding* on faith. What's wrong with you? That's so boring and stiff and preachy."

But if you've found the Christian faith, then you've found what's real, true, and good. Most people are desperately searching for what you have. Stay strong and know that your faith in God is more important than any criticism you may receive.

WHAT IF ADAM DIDN'T HAVE A BELLY BUTTON?

DOUBT AND FAITH IN COLLEGE

SITUATION

When you were younger, being a Christian was easy.
You sang songs about being in the Lord's army and learned the "Deep and Wide" hand motions. It wasn't clear what the song "Deep and Wide" was all about, but you were pretty sure it had something to do with Jesus.

In high school you were involved in a great youth group, and your youth pastor's talks inspired you to get closer to God. But now that you're in college, you're starting to look at things a little more closely. What is heaven really? And what is hell? Are we predestined? Or are we solely responsible for our own salvation? Does God love all sinners the same, or are some sins worse than others? Was Jonah swallowed by a whale or a really big fish?

Did Adam have a belly button? He wouldn't need one. Belly buttons have everything to do with umbilical cords, and Adam didn't have a mother. So why would he need a belly button? But wouldn't he look really freaky without one?

All of these questions are starting to rattle your faith. You wonder, *What do I really believe?*

Did Adam have a belly button?

SYMPTOMS

You're afraid they'll kick you out of church if you say the words *Bible* and *not literal* in the same sentence. You feel as though you're having all of these doubts with no one to talk to. Every time you bring up something you're curious about, they just laugh it off and say something like, "You're beginning to sound like one of those psycho left-wing liberals."

You're extremely confused in science class.
Since coming to college, you've learned about other ways of explaining the universe, evolution, existence, and the meaning of life. Most of your high school teachers were pleasant and understanding of your Christian worldview. But in college, some professors say horrible things about the Christian faith just to push your buttons.

You met a cute boy from a different denomination and wonder if interfaith dating is wrong.
Now that you think about it, is interdenominational dating actually interfaith dating? Pastors love to joke about other denominations, but you wonder, *What do different denominations really believe? Are they wrong? Am I wrong?*

SOLUTION

Step 1: Don't stop with doubt.
J. R. R. Tolkien famously wrote "Not all those who wander are lost." Just because you're doubting some things and trying to find answers doesn't mean you're sinning. It's perfectly okay to be confused and stay up nights trying to find answers to important questions. Having these questions and choosing not to ignore them will ultimately build your faith. Ignoring such questions will make you cynical.

Step 2: Know the difference between the absolutes of the faith and nonabsolute ideas.

It's easy to get overwhelmed by various interpretations and views within Christianity and the church. It's also easy to treat every argument with a fellow Christian like it's you versus Satan.

There are absolutes of the faith that all Christians should believe, such as Jesus is the Son of God. Other concepts are only opinions or interpretations, such as the existence of Adam's belly button. Doctrines such as predestination, gifts of the spirit, and interpretations of certain Scriptures fall into the nonabsolute category. Scripture includes absolutes and other issues that are matters of preference. This is why knowing when to blow off an argument or dig in your heels is important to learn in college.

FURTHER READING

Some great books that build faith from an intellectual point of view are *Mere Christianity* by C. S. Lewis, *Evidence That Demands a Verdict* by Josh McDowell, and pretty much anything written by Ravi Zacharias or Lee Strobel.

Any book introducing you to theology might help you decipher the difference between a foundational Christian idea and an opinion. *Who Needs Theology?* by Stanley Grenz and Roger Olson is a good beginning.

203

WE'RE ALL JESUS FREAKS
SURVIVING THE CHRISTIAN COLLEGE

SITUATION

It's five minutes until midnight.
You and your best friend are sprinting across campus. If someone were watching, they'd assume you were being chased—maybe by a cop, or a rabid dog, or some sort of psycho. But it's none of those things.

In fact, no one is chasing you at all.

You're running because you attend a Christian college, which means you have curfew. And in five minutes you're going to be late. Again. This time being late will mean 10 demerits and a $50 fine. You've already missed chapel this week, and you got busted for wearing your skirt too high and your pants too low. College is hard enough, but going to a Christian college with all of these rules is nearly overwhelming.

Going to a Christian College may involve sprinting to make curfew.

SYMPTOMS

You get busted for watching an R-rated movie.
You're having a bunch of friends over to your dorm room to watch *Braveheart*. You've just settled in, turned on the TV, and hit PLAY on the DVD remote, when the RA busts in. Everyone flees the room like high school students running from a party when the cops arrive. And now you're left to explain what you were doing. "I didn't think watching an

R-rated movie was that big a deal," you say. "We were even going to fast-forward through the sex scene."

You didn't know there was such a thing as co-ed dorms.

Your friend at another college is telling you a story about how she and her boyfriend were hanging out in her room. You ask, "How did you hide him from your RA?"

"I didn't," she says. "We have co-ed dorms."

This is shocking and a little bit scary to you.

"So you can have guys in your rooms whenever you want?" you ask as you imagine guys and girls walking around in some sort of utopian dorm society.

You hear someone singing a Christian song in the shower.

As you walk by the bathroom on your dorm floor, you hear someone belting out, "What will people think, when they hear that I'm a Jesus freak?" in the shower. When you run into that person a little while later, you say, "Was that you I heard singing 'Jesus Freak'?"

"Yeah," she answers.

"Well, um, you have a good voice," you reply.

"Thank you," she says. "I'm trying out for *Michael W. Smith: The Musical*. I hope I get the part of Amy Grant."

Chapel isn't anything like your home church.

You have required chapel services a couple times a week. But the music they play is different from what you're used to hearing at your home church. And the band plays the same four songs during every chapel service. The speakers preach about things you've never heard your pastor speak on, such as money or political issues, and the style of preaching is a lot more bombastic. You thought you'd like going to a Christian college because you'd get to worship with your friends, but you feel like a foreigner in these services.

You're sick of Christians.
It was exciting to think about being around other Christians when you first thought about going to a Christian college. It would be a natural community. But soon you became tired of hanging around nothing but Christians all the time. You call your campus "the bubble." You feel like everyone belongs to the same political party. And if one more person calls you "brother" or "sister," you're going to be sick.

SOLUTION

We're all in this together.
One great thing about Christian colleges is that all of the rules and requirements create instant community. Loneliness doesn't happen so often when all of your friends are trying to survive curfew, dress code, chapel, and classes.

So enjoy the community. Have everyone from your floor wear polka-dotted bow ties to chapel. Find a midnight prayer meeting. Memorize the book of Leviticus and use it to correct your friends when they don't study hard enough or they spend too much time staring at girls. These are the types of things you can't do at any other type of college in America.[3] So do stuff like this and enjoy your Christian college life.

---

3. At least not without facing a medieval amount of ridicule.

Find ways to have fun.

If your dorm has a curfew, lock yourself in at night and have manicure and pedicure parties in one of your rooms. Hold a rock-paper-scissors tournament where the winner gets to be king of the dorm room for a day. Turn a hallway into a Slip 'N Slide. If you're going to school in the South, see who can knock over the most bowling pins with a giant catfish. All of these activities are what we call good clean Christian fun.

Avoid cynicism.

Sometimes it's more difficult to graduate as a Christian from a Christian college than from a secular one. Not only do you get a front row seat to the weaknesses of other students, pastors, and administrators; but some of the systems of a Christian college can turn your stomach regarding Christianity in general.

College is a good time to learn how flawed we really are. As much as your roommate, RA, best friend, or pastor seem to have it all together, they also have their flaws. You may even observe a few of these flaws in person and think, *I knew he couldn't be that holy.* And you're right. Give yourself a hand.

But you're not that holy either. None of us are. The sooner you learn that, the less cynicism you'll face.

Celebrate discipline.

We know. This is something your dad would probably say. But part of college is learning to have structure in your life.

And some college rules help you to create that structure. So embrace it. After all, some of the unique challenges and rules of going to a Christian college are what make it fun.

Enjoy the chapel services for what they are. Look at curfew as a way of learning to hit deadlines. View your dress code as an excuse to learn to tie a tie. If you're trying to coast through college by only *appearing* to obey all the rules, then you're probably going to become really bitter when you get called out for something. And no one likes a bitter Christian college student.

But people have a deep respect for someone who's not afraid to stand out for his faith and hold to his convictions.

204

SLEEPING IN UNTIL 3 P.M. ON A SUNDAY

FINDING A CHURCH

SITUATION

You just woke up—it's Sunday ... 3 p.m.
Since birth you've never been able to sleep in on a Sunday without Mom or Dad trying to drag you out of bed singing, "RISE AND SHINE, AND GIVE GOD THE GLORY, GLORY!"

But this morning (or is it afternoon?), you're starting to miss your home church. You miss walking into the building on Sunday and hearing the greeters say, "Well, don't you look sharp today!" You still don't know what that means— *look sharp*—but it was nice to hear.

When you found your seat, you knew a lot of the people sitting around you. You knew what kind of music the worship pastor would start with, and you knew exactly when to sit and when to stand.

You also knew everyone in the youth group and the pastor who told funny jokes. And you looked forward to having lunch after church each week with your girlfriend's family.

Now you don't know where to go to church. *Do they even have churches in this town?* you think.

SYMPTOMS

You haven't heard anyone call you "brother" or "sister" for at least a month.
You miss having deep conversations with other Christians who know where you're coming from. You miss the smiles and—most of all—your youth group where everyone knows your name or at least refers to you as "bro" or "sis."

You can't remember the words to "Amazing Grace."
You grew up knowing all the songs and the answers to the Sunday school questions about Jesus. But college is beginning to mess with that. You've never met so many professors and classmates who are opposed to Christianity. Doubt is breathing down your neck, and you feel like there's no one you can talk to. The other day you were humming "Amazing Grace," and suddenly you couldn't remember what comes after "How sweet the...." *Is it song, sand, or sound?*

Church seems like a part of your old life.
You wonder what your youth pastor or parents would say if they knew what you did last weekend. Not going to church has pulled you toward the things you thought you'd never try in college. You're feeling ashamed that you haven't been to church in a long time, and you wonder if you've passed the point of no return.

Church used to feel like home, but now you're not sure. You think, *What if I don't fit in anymore? What if all of a sudden the worship music annoys me? And do I really look like all of the other people at church? I read Kierkegaard. They read Osteen.* You're starting to wonder if they'd call you a backslider. And what if they did? Maybe church is just something you *used* to do.

SOLUTION

There are lots of churches.
With your brand-new college point of view, it can be easy to believe that you've moved beyond church. The people at church are kind of into their own things. They don't think like you do. They don't know where you're at.

Yet, while it's easy to think like this—it's also wrong.

The reality is there are many churches: Churches with Bible studies and sermons for the intellectually elite, churches with groups of people your age, churches with top-quality musicians, churches focused on liturgy, and churches focused on practical teaching from the Scriptures for your everyday life.

The problem isn't finding a church—it's finding the *right* church. And finding a church in college is tricky *because* there are so many options. Should you go to a church on campus or somewhere with an actual church building? Can you meet with a group of friends and read the Bible, or do you need an actual pastor to have church?

Here's a list of the types of churches that typically exist in a college town and the good and the bad of each one:

The On-Campus Ministry
There are probably numerous Christian clubs and ministries that meet right on your campus. Navigators, InterVarsity Christian Fellowship, Campus Crusade for Christ, and the Baptist Student Union have all been around for years, just to name a few.

The Good: On-campus ministries are the most similar to a youth group. If you liked the silly games involving spoons on strings and food fights, then you'll love on-campus ministries. They're fun and easy to plug into.

The Bad: There's a lot of turnover in these groups. The group of people you enjoy hanging out with in the fall might be totally different in the spring. Also, you probably aren't thinking four years down the road; but after you graduate from college, you'll be kicked out of these groups and have to start all over. (No one wants to see a creepy 30-year-old with a mustache playing "pass the spoon" with the freshmen girls.)

The Local Church
No matter what the denomination, a local church consists of young and old people who gather to worship Jesus. Much like choosing a college, though, it's good to know what you're looking for in a local church. Are you interested in studying in-depth theology? Would you like to attend a church that focuses on the arts? Or a church that can help you with the daily struggles of life? Again, some churches will do certain things better than others, so decide what you're looking for and what will help you feel at home.

The Good: It's stable. There are potlucks and plenty of free food for visitors. You can find older mentors to meet with. And after college you can remain an integral part of the church. People in the congregation will want you to stay involved after you graduate. You can go to that church at any point in your life, whether you're a single business-man or married with a couple of toddlers running around. This is church for the long haul.

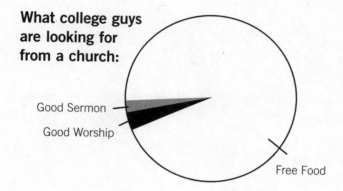

What college guys are looking for from a church:

Good Sermon

Good Worship

Free Food

The Bad: Local churches are notorious for not offering much for college students. They have great ministries for teenagers, kids, and old people, but nothing for college-age students.

When trying to find a church that will be the best fit for the cool, young hipster that you are, avoid any churches that advertise with more than one dove, globe, or American flag in their logo.

The Dorm Room Group

These groups are typically created informally and may consist of just you and a few buddies who like to get a large pepperoni pizza and talk about the Bible.

There's nothing like a hellfire and brimstone sermon in your dorm room.

The Good: Nothing says community like a dorm room group. They can allow for the deepest friendships and most sincere accountability you've ever known.

The Bad: These groups can have cult tendencies. Seriously. Your "leader" may or may not know more theology than a biblically trained monkey. If this is your only source of church, prepare to get a little confused because all members get to share their opinions in these groups.

A dorm room group is a great way to strengthen your faith, but it shouldn't be your primary church. If this is the only place you're being taught from Scripture, then you need to realize that your leader could be making up many of her (or his—guys are especially guilty of making up stuff) opinions on Scripture, the Trinity, heaven, hell, God, Jesus, and Satan on the spot.

205

IS REVELATION BEFORE OR AFTER GENESIS?

YOU CAN'T REMEMBER THE LAST TIME YOU READ YOUR BIBLE

SITUATION

College hasn't been going very well in the spiritual department.
You're running around like a chicken with your head cut off as you finish assignments, work at your part-time job, and add items to your to-do list. Still, you want to turn over a new leaf in spending time with God, and you have great plans for the morning. The alarm is set to go off early, and your Bible is opened to the book of Psalms for a planned morning of what you like to call "Christ and Coffee."

But just as you're falling asleep, the fellas on the second floor wake you up and challenge you to a couple games of Texas hold 'em. The game is epic, and you win six boxes of Swiss Cake Rolls.

Three hours later the alarm is going off, and you can't remember why in the world you set it that early. You go back to sleep as your Bible still lays open to Psalms.

It's a lot harder to have a devotional time
after an all night game of Texas hold 'em.

SYMPTOMS

It'll take a half can of Pledge to get the dust off your Bible.
Now that you think of it ... where *is* your Bible? Did you
lose it at youth group last winter? Did you forget to pack it
for college? You try to remember the last time you read your
Bible, but you end up staring blankly at the wall.

**Scheduling time with God is like trying to get a sit-down
meeting with the president.**
You want to spend time with God. You'd also like to meet
Johnny Depp and someday have a line of cologne or perfume
named after you. Why not dream big? Those things seem
about as likely to happen as having a steady devotional time.

You feel like it takes the mental training of a monk to be able to concentrate during prayers or while reading your Bible.

Your times of devotion feel as though they're getting nowhere. You start reading a passage from Obadiah, only to let your mind wander to how cool the name Obadiah would be for a band. You're the lead singer, and the crowd is chanting your name. You take off your guitar and throw yourself off the stage and into the waiting arms of the audience and crowd surf. It's so awesome! Just then your roommate walks by and asks, "Dude, why are you chanting your own name?"

SOLUTION

Develop a hunger for God.

If you're reading this chapter and are actually taking it to heart, the last thing you need is someone pointing a finger at you and saying, "You need to have a quiet time with God." You already *know* you should be reading the Bible and having great prayer times, but there's a lack of interest. When you look at the real situation, what you need to develop is a hunger for God.

If you're hungry for food and your belly is growling, no one has to tell you to eat something. You want to eat. You'll make time to eat even if it's just a bagel on the way to work.

The same is true of your spiritual hunger to spend time with God. If you're spiritually hungry, you'll find time for God.

Don't eat spiritual junk food.

There's an endless list of things that are straight up sins. (Refer to the Ten Commandments and the rest of your Bible for some examples.) But for starters, how about underage drinking, one-night stands, and stealing someone's term paper and claiming it's yours.

Sometimes it's not the blatant sin that keeps you away from God, though. Sometimes it's the subtle time-wasters — TV, video games, spending three days straight on Facebook — that keep you from some good old-fashioned quiet time.

We're not saying you can't watch TV. In fact, if you've read this entire book, then you've seen how many TV shows and movies we've watched. But at the same time, once or twice a week it's good to go home early, turn off prime time television, stop reading status updates, and just spend some time in prayer and Scripture.

Put it on the calendar.

We've talked about this a lot, but college is about more responsibility. Your classes are more intense and so are the sports you play. And your girlfriend or boyfriend, well … they're incredibly intense. Oftentimes it's not that you *don't* want to spend time with God, it's just that suddenly another week has gone by and it never happened.

So schedule the time. The same way you know when you have to be at class or study group or practice, know when your devotional time is scheduled on the calendar. It doesn't have to be a huge chunk of time. You don't have to read the entire book of Revelation. (In fact, we'd strongly recommend against reading the entire book in one sitting.) The important thing is that you're consistent and you don't break the time you've scheduled with God.

It might be as small as reading a chapter every day or reflecting on one verse, but it won't just happen by itself. And after a while it'll become part of your routine, and you'll wonder why you ever had to force yourself to do it in the first place.

Find a friend.
If you've lost your appetite for spending time with God, maybe a friend could help you regain some of that lost passion. Pick a book of the Bible together and talk about it as you read the chapters. It's amazing what insights and encouragement two people can receive when they read the Bible together or talk about their times of devotion.

Don't ignore the hunger pangs.
God prompts us to spend time with him. Don't ignore these promptings. Food makes such a good analogy for time spent with God. If you don't eat when your body feels hungry, it gets sick and malnourished. The same thing can happen with your spiritual self.

Your soul needs to be fed.

If you feel prompted to spend time with God, there's probably a reason. Follow that prompting. And as you respond more and more, the desire to spend time with God will increase. If you feel like reading your Bible under a tree by the campus pond, don't get distracted by a pro-test, a club meeting, an invitation to get another afternoon snack in the cafeteria, or whatever else pops up on your way to that tree. Stay focused, keep walking, and don't stop until you're finally sitting under the tree, looking at the clouds, and pondering the One who created all of this in the first place.

PART (DATING SITUATIONS) 3

(PREREQUISITE 3: TYPES OF COLLEGE SINGLES)

BEFORE YOU BEGIN READING "DATING SITUATIONS" . . .

YOU SHOULD KNOW THAT YOUR COLLEGE YEARS MAY BE THE BEST TIME TO MEET A YOUNG, ELIGIBLE, AND VERY SPECIAL SOMEONE WITH WHOM YOU CAN SHARE THE REST OF YOUR LIFE.

All around you are attractive, capable, and smart people with similar interests.

But dating in college is a whole different ballgame than dating in high school. The people are obviously older, have higher expectations, and play for bigger stakes. So before we dive into the dating situations that you'll face in your college life, we want you to know more about the types of singles you'll meet.

There are a few stereotypical Christian singles that you might be. Like we've said in other sections, no person is exactly one stereotype, but everyone has tendencies toward one or more of these types. So it's important that you decide which one best represents you and be aware of the good and the bad facets of that type.

In addition, you can read about the stereotypes of the opposite sex to help you stay clear of those that might cause you problems.

We'll begin with the guys.

THE TYPES — *GUYS*

THE STALKER

While some might call it "stalking," when it comes to relationships, you prefer more positive words such as *perusing*, *researching*, and *persistence*. You may do some *researching* so you can show up at the same parties as the girl you like, or perhaps you'll leave secret little gifts and notes in places where she'll find them.

When the time is right, you'll find out her favorite band and buy two tickets for an upcoming concert. Then you'll just happen to bump into her on the way to class one day and say, "Hey, I came across two tickets to the [*insert the name of her favorite band here*] concert tonight. Would you like to join me?"

"Wow, you got tickets for that concert?" she replies. "That's really great, but I have my study group tonight. I wish they were tickets for tomorrow night."

You say, "Great! I just happen to have two tickets for tomorrow night's show, too — in case you couldn't make it tonight."

She is now flattered, but a little scared. As the conversation progresses, she feels even more scared because you seem to know her class schedule, her favorite movies, and every boyfriend she's had since the third grade.

Finally she asks, "How do you know all of this?"

"Because I care," you say in the most smothering tone imaginable.

The Good: Most people are afraid to ask someone out, but you have no problems there. This is a really good thing—and especially in the Christian world where a guy who takes the initiative to ask a girl out is becoming an endangered species.

The Bad: The Stalker can be smothering. Part of what makes a relationship exciting in the beginning is the mystery of getting to know the other person and discovering your feelings for each other. There's no mystery with the Stalker. It just feels like you're in a rush to find someone. And finding someone to commit to should never be forced. If you're the Stalker, allow more time for a girl to get to know you without pushing the relationship too hard and too fast.

THE PRINCE

You're called the Prince because a harem of girls is always hanging around you. A half-dozen girls call you their best friend. Another half-dozen believe you'll be their boyfriend as soon as you make things "official." Drama follows you wherever you go, and you wouldn't have it any other way.

The Good: If you're the Prince, you probably have really cool hair and a good sense of style. You can easily relate to girls, and you feel relaxed and confident around the opposite sex.

The Bad: The Prince has to realize that he's playing with a bunch of girls' hearts and turning them against each other. You can dress it up however you want, but this is the plain and simple truth. There's a reason why drama follows the Prince — *he* is *the drama*. If you're the Prince, be ready to have Define the Relationship talks with any girl you're befriending. Telling a girl that this relationship is only a friendship will probably hurt her feelings and may even end the friendship. But this talk is bound to happen. It's just a matter of time.

THE "KISSED DATING GOOD-BYE" GUY

You vowed never to date. Maybe there are valid reasons for this decision; maybe there are unhealed emotional wounds. But whatever the reason, you say things like, "Dating is a waste of time," or "When I find my dream girl, I'll know," or "Why would I waste all of my energy on a relationship?"

Lots of your friends roll their eyes when you say things like this. But when they're wrecked for weeks over their latest breakups, you have to bite your tongue to keep from saying, "I told you so."

The Good: You're a person of conviction, and you're sticking to those convictions.

The Bad: You need to figure out the real reason you're refusing to date anyone. If you're legitimately waiting on God, that's great. If dating isn't the most important thing to you right now, that's also great. However, the "Kissed Dating Good-bye" Guy (KDGG) can easily flaunt his convictions in other people's faces. And that makes his friends want to *not* kiss punching people in the face good-bye.

If you're the KDGG, then be humble about your convictions. And it's also okay to give yourself a season of time in which you're kissing dating good-bye ... and then you can kiss it hello again.

The College Christian Singles' Paradox

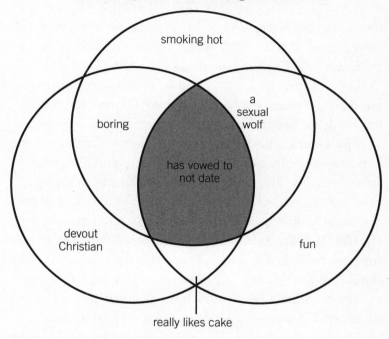

smoking hot

a sexual wolf

boring

has vowed to not date

devout Christian

fun

really likes cake

THE TYPES—*GIRLS*

THE JEZEBEL

Long before women were stabbing each other in the back on reality television, there was Jezebel. Jezebel was this woman in the Old Testament who messed with every guy she came across and used her feminine powers to try to get them into trouble. (We're talking false gods, idols, sexual tyranny ... you get the idea.) Chaos followed her wherever she went, and she made lots of enemies. She got a really bad rap.[1]

If you're the Jezebel, then other girls don't like you very much because you're always dating someone new and dropping the old ones like flies. You'll be kind to, flirt with, and smile at a guy if he has something you want.

Deep down, the Jezebel is probably a wonderful person, but there are many guys on campus who'd use a lot of different words to describe her.

The Good: The Jezebel often makes enemies, but she never lacks confidence. This is why guys and girls react so strongly to her. She possesses a self-confidence and assuredness that's gotten her ahead in many areas of her life, and she's not about to slow down when it comes to relationships.

The Bad: The Jezebel often finds her self-worth in attracting guys because she doesn't know who she is in Christ. She should read Scriptures that offer God's view of her. If you're the Jezebel, God wants you to know that you are his beloved daughter. Try memorizing some verses to combat these false attacks on your identity. (Good starters are John 1:12, John 15:15, Romans 8:1–2, and Philippians 4:13.) Find out who you are in Christ first, and then take some time alone to listen to God's truth about you.

---

1. To see how truly frightening she was (we're talking the worst imaginable reality TV star kind of frightening) read 1 Kings chapters 18-21 and 2 Kings 9.

THE MISSIONARY

The Missionary shows up at church every couple of weeks with a guy she met at school, near the bus stop, or even at a bar. If you're the Missionary, then you're attracted to the bad guy. But you believe there's a good reason you're attracted to him: You can see who he *really* is deep down.

This is why you bring the new guy to church and tell yourself he'll change his bad-guy ways. You may also believe you're his only hope of salvation. As soon as he accepts Christ and stops being so mean to puppies, he's going to make a great boyfriend.

The Good: If you're the Missionary, you truly care for other people. And you can see the good in any guy. Sure the one you're looking at right now refers to women as "arm candy," and he drinks six-packs on the way to work. But you see the best in him. *He's going to build orphanages in Africa one day*, you think.

The Bad: The Missionary needs to understand that she's not responsible for changing people. Sure a bad guy will come to church and act good in order to be with a girl. This doesn't mean he's actually changing. He's just trying to impress her.

But most importantly, you need to understand that although you may be some light in his life, you're not his only hope for becoming a Christian.

THE ROYAL HIGHNESS

She's waiting for Prince Charming—that is, the hot pre-med student who plays the guitar, spends his summers with orphans, and has also never dated anyone. If you're the Royal Highness, then you're unobtainable. It's what makes you so attractive. All the guys secretly love you, but none of them would ever show they're attracted to you because you'd quickly shoot them down.

The Good: It's okay to know what you want in a relationship. If you're the Royal Highness, then you know *exactly* what you're looking for. And knowing the type of person you do (and don't) want to be with will help you not to settle for someone.

The Bad: You also need to hold your expectations loosely. You're not going to date someone who meets all 200 points on your fairytale checklist. You're going to be dating a real guy who may not have perfect teeth, good shoes, flowing blond hair, and a cute soul patch. He may not even play acoustic guitar like you imagined he would.

Every guy has good days and bad days. He's going to grow in some areas and falter in others. It's an asset to know what type of relationship and person you're looking for. Just don't hold on to that list so tightly that you miss a chance at someone special or a great relationship.

301

HOW TO MEET THE SMOKING HOT CHRISTIAN OF YOUR DREAMS

A PRACTICAL INTRODUCTION TO DATING FOR THE COLLEGE CHRISTIAN

SITUATION

It's love at first sight.

You're sitting in the Wednesday night college group for Christians on your campus. Your eyes are closed, and your hands are folded nicely during a time of sharing prayer requests and praying for each other.

Then this very attractive hottie stands up to pray, and suddenly you're daydreaming and getting all starry-eyed. Your thoughts trail from how cute this person is to how amazing this hottie's Christian faith must be that he or she is able to stand up in front of everyone and pray for a friend's grandmother.

Wow, how can you meet her?

How can you find out his name?

You don't know. But now you have a goal. All you can think is ... *Wow!*

SYMPTOMS

You dress like it's Saturday night every time you go to Campus Crusade.
Guys, you wear your favorite blazer and shoes. Girls, you wear that dress that makes you feel smoking hot. You even ask your friends, "Does this dress make me look smoking hot?" If your friends hesitate, then you change and make sure you wear the right dress. You get dressed up every time you go to Campus Crusade (or any time you could possibly run into the person you're crushing on). You even go to the gym dressed like you're going to a spa in Maui.

You stalk his friends.
You know who his best friends are, and you start hanging out with them. You'll see them at the cafeteria or on campus, and you'll strike up a casual conversation. Thirty seconds in, though, and you're grilling them with questions about him:
   "What music does he like?"
   "What are his hobbies?"
   "What's his favorite candy bar?"
   "What kind of girls does he like?"
   You're not trying to be a stalker, but you know how competitive the dating world is. If you're going to stand a chance, then you need to find out all that you can.

You're sitting in the bleachers.
The number one symptom is that you like the person, but she doesn't know you like her. It's kind of like a junior

high dance. You wanted to talk to the girls, but you were too nervous. So you spent the whole evening sitting in the bleachers with your friends.

Well, you're in college now.

It's time to get out of the bleachers.

So walk across that gym floor while the disco ball twirls and ask the girl to dance. You can do it! But if you're not sure what to do next, keep reading for your game plan.

SOLUTION

WARNING: The authors of this book assume that you have a real faith and wouldn't try to coerce guys or girls to like you by manipulating their faith. This chapter presents tools to get the attention of a hot Christian guy or girl. These tools can be very dangerous if placed in the wrong hands, so be careful not to leave this book just lying around.

Step 1: Bring your Bible to the meeting.
There's a modern proverb that says, "Be who you want to date." If you want to date a strong Christian, you have to be a strong Christian. Bringing your Bible to the meeting shouldn't be a fake gesture to get that Christian hottie's attention. It should be a real sign of your faith. Hopefully the person you're interested in will notice your faith and this quality will attract her to you.

Step 2: Location, location, location.
During the meeting you can't possibly make your move from across the room. Sit behind him after worship but before

the talk. At this point in most services, there's usually a time for meeting and greeting. He'll probably turn around during this time, so make a good first impression! Smile, say your name, and remember his name. Then move right on to meeting someone else.

If at all possible (without being awkward), position yourself at his side toward the end of the meeting. Many meetings end with a prayer circle in which you can hold hands—you'll be in a perfect place for steps three and four.

Step 3: Start up a conversation immediately following the service.

Easy conversation starters include, "Wasn't worship powerful?" and "The speaker is so funny." If you remember his name from the meet and greet, say it a few times during the course of the conversation. Another modern proverb says, "A person's name is the most beautiful sound to him."

Step 4: Invite her to go to dinner with a group of your friends after the meeting.

If all goes well in step three, then you'll need some more time together. Christians love to eat food after meetings. Tell her that you and some of your friends are going out for dinner at a nearby restaurant. (Note: This can't seem like you're asking her on a date. If it even smells like a date, she may shy away from the idea, thinking you're being too forward.)

If she agrees, then kindly excuse yourself from the conversation and catch up with your friends. Tell them they all have to go out to dinner *right now* because the Christian hottie said yes. If your friends hesitate, tell them you'll buy them an appetizer. (A small price to pay for the chance of a lifetime!)

302

AVOIDING A NIGHTMARE DATE
PLANNING THE PERFECT FIRST DATE

SITUATION

You're getting ready for the *big first date*.
Your roommate is setting you up with her boyfriend's cous-
in's friend, and she's told you all about how this guy is
unlike any other. You've never been on a blind date before,
and you're wondering what this will be like. It felt a little
awkward and superficial to do this, but before you agreed
to go on the date, you asked to see a picture of the guy.

He was cute.

No Prince Charming, but he's an attractive guy nonethe-
less. As the time approaches for him to pick you up, you're
feeling a little nervous. But your roomie keeps reminding
you about how fun and cool this guy is. What kind of date
will it be? Hopefully it won't become one of the disasters
described below. But if you do find yourself on one of these
nightmare dates, read the solutions carefully.

SYMPTOMS — TYPES OF BAD DATES

The *Let's Get Married* Date
This date has either one or both of you moving at the speed
of light in the emotional department. The fact that this is
a first date doesn't stop you from asking questions like,

"Where do you see us in two years?" or "Do you think I meet any of your criteria for a Christian spouse?"

The *When Will This Date End?* Date
This date has no plan and no direction, and it leaves you standing around saying things like, "Well, what were *you* thinking of doing tonight?"

The *Awkward Silence* Date
You're trying to think of something to say. But now so much time has passed since you last said anything, your date is probably expecting you to say something pretty profound. Finally, you ask a question and get a one-word response. Wow, this date is awkward.

The *Verbal Vomit* Date
This date is the exact opposite of the Awkward Silence Date. It involves one person sharing her entire history and emotional baggage in one run-on sentence. You nod and smile as though you care, but all you asked her was, "How was your day?" It's the most involved life story you've ever heard.

The *Why Do I Need A Shirt?* Date
This date starts off great, but then someone gets a little too close. Maybe it's the guy who yawns and puts his arm around you, then asks, "Do I have something in my eye?" Or suddenly he takes off his shirt for no apparent reason, like he's Matthew McConaughey. And he starts saying things like, "Let's go back to my place."

He's cute, but now all of the cuteness is overshadowed by his creepiness. You wonder if any girl has ever had the courage to say to him, "You might be cute if you weren't so creepy." Maybe you'll be the first.

Beware the guys who take off their shirts at the movie theater.

SOLUTION

Be friends first.
A lot of awkwardness is alleviated if you already feel confident and can be yourself around the person. Dating as a Christian in college should be about finding someone you love to be around and can fall in love with.

Ask your date about her.
A first date isn't the time to unload your baggage upon an unsuspecting person. If awkward silences make you ner-

vous, plan some questions ahead of time. Here are a few that can break the ice on any date:

- What are your hobbies?
- What's your favorite TV show?
- Who's your hero?
- What's your major? Why did you choose it?
- Do you like camping and hiking or malls and hotels?
- Who do you think would win a kick boxing cage match: Abraham Lincoln or George Washington?

A date should have a plan.
If it's a dinner date, what are you going to do after dinner? You need a plan. If the date goes well throughout dinner, what are you going to do next—just sit in the restaurant lobby and repeatedly say to each other, "Well, what do *you* want to do?"

Guys, when you're taking out a girl, you should have in mind a place you want to take her after the meal and a backup plan if that first idea fails.

Excuse yourself to make a phone call and never go back.
Let's say you're on a disaster of a date. Besides being awkward, you feel a little creeped out. Be nice, but know that you have the right to end the date at any time or just leave. There are a million things you can say to end a date, just be firm.

A Christian Girl's Dilemma

Guys that ask me out

creepy guys

old guys

stalkers

Guys that will never ask me out

Movie stars

Christian guys

303

RING BY SPRING OR
JUST FRIENDS?

DTR (DEFINING THE RELATIONSHIP)

SITUATION

Are you guys a couple?

Just about everyone has been asking you this question. Your friends, your parents, your chemistry professor— everyone wants to know, "What's the deal with you two?" You both admit that you like spending time with each other. That much is obvious.

Then one night you're watching a movie with a group of friends, and you end up sitting by each other on the couch. It wasn't planned, but you're not sad it happened either. Everyone else is totally focused on the movie, but you can't stop thinking about the person you're sitting next to—like the fact that your legs are touching. (And then you suddenly flash back to dinner and realize what a bad idea it was to eat that garlic roll.)

That's when it happens. Both of you plunge a hand into the popcorn bowl at the same time, and you let your hands linger in the bowl for a moment longer than they should. There's so much electricity in that bowl that it feels like any unpopped kernels may explode.

You can't ignore it anymore. Something's going on. You like him—this is more than just being friends. But do you both feel the same way? Are you going to bring it up? Will he freak out and think you're too smothering or controlling for trying to define what you have?

It's a risk you have to take. Finally, when the movie is finished and everyone's either gone home or out to Denny's, it's just the two of you. You say goodnight and are about to part ways when you ask, "Are we a couple?"

SYMPTOMS

Your friends refer to you as Mr. and Mrs. So-and-So.
A good sign that it's time to define the relationship is when everyone assumes you're in one. When the two of you walk by, they sing, "Here comes the bride!" and throw rice at you.[2] And girls start fighting over who gets to be the bridesmaid.

You turn into an MMA fighter every time another guy talks to her.
Maybe you're not convinced that you should have a romantic relationship. After all, you're *just friends* who talk on the phone every now and again. But then you see another guy talking with her. He's wearing a ridiculous muscle shirt, and *your* girl giggles every time he tells a joke. She brushes her fingertips across his shoulder and says, "You're *so* funny!"

---

2. Please don't actually throw rice at anyone. We've just learned that birds explode when they eat rice. So throw birdseed instead. But whatever you do, *don't* throw Alka-Seltzer tablets on the ground. That stuff goes nuclear when it gets inside a bird's digestive system.

303: RING BY SPRING OR JUST FRIENDS?   (127)

That's when you run across the cafeteria and slap him in the face with your tray. Once he's face down on the ground, you hunch over him, bend his arm behind him, and growl, "Never talk to her again. Next time I won't be so nice." Then everyone cheers for you because you're the bravest guy on campus and you stood up for yourself and your dream girl.

Okay, you don't actually do that.

But that's what you feel like doing. Maybe instead of taking out your aggression on another guy, you should just define the relationship you have.

"A date? I didn't think we were on a date. I just thought we were carpooling."

As he picks you up for dinner, you mention something about how nice this date will be. But he responds with the above sentence—or something to that effect. You want to scream, "WHAT?! 'Carpooling' to dinner and a movie is a *date*, buddy!" Instead, you just sit in the car and listen to the CD you made for him, wondering what in the world is going on here.

You practice writing your first name with his last name.

Your name is Kelly Edwards. But for some reason, you've started writing *Kelly Anderson* on everything because you imagine yourself married to Steve Anderson, that adorable guy you sit next to in three different classes.[3] You can't

---

3. Guys, please don't write your first name with her last name. It doesn't work like that. Well, you could imagine your name hyphenated, like Steven Anderson-Edwards. But that's still kind of weird.

help yourself. *What if we somehow did get married?* you think. *Wow! That name looks good*, you think as you look at all of the *Kelly Anderson*s written on your paper. You even think *Steve and Kelly Anderson* would look pretty good on a wedding invitation or family Christmas card.

SOLUTION

Hint at your feelings.
Your first impulse in this type of relationship may be to come on too strong. Sometimes it's good to give the other person space to know where he or she is at. She may have just gotten out of another relationship and isn't ready to get into a new one. Or he might not be ready for a serious commitment.

The only way to know for sure is to start talking about it. Hint at it. You don't have to come on strong at first. Don't say things like, "I could totally see us married a year from now." But let that person know you're ready for a relationship. See where she is. Talk. Explore your feelings and hers.

Don't worry about losing the friendship.
One of the bigger reasons why relationships don't get defined is because you think you're going to lose the friendship. Let's be honest: You *could* lose the friendship. Things might get a little weird between you. But if your feelings for the other person are strong, you're probably going to lose the friendship anyway. It will happen when something gets

weird—like he starts dating another person—or when you risk it and put your feelings out there.

Don't get strung along.

It's easy to compromise what you want out of the relationship just to make the other person happy. Don't tell yourself, *Well, she's not ready for a relationship, so why am I forcing it?* If you've been in this ambiguous state for a while (see preceding symptoms) and nothing is happening, then you have two options. One: Keep letting yourself get dragged along until the other person either caves in or starts dating someone else. Two: Define the relationship!

304

WHERE EXACTLY IS THIRD BASE?
YOUR PHYSICAL RELATIONSHIP

SITUATION

It's 10 p.m. on a Saturday.
You and your boyfriend are studying for a math test when he makes a joke about how acute triangles are adorable. *What a sweet joke*, you think. And then you think, *He's really funny and charming and hot*. He's wearing just a hint of cologne—you didn't even notice it before, but now it's like sweet nectar calling you near.

Suddenly he's irresistible.

And the math books get pushed to the floor.

You end up in a five-hour make-out session without so much as a break for water. On the way back to your dorm room, you rehearse your cover story should your roommate ask, "Why are you getting back so late from your so-called study session?"

But is this going to be an ongoing problem? You think, *Did I cross a line? Am I going to cross a line? What sort of line should there be? What's a safe boundary for us? Did we go past second base? And where exactly is third base?*

304: WHERE EXACTLY IS THIRD BASE?   (131)

SYMPTOMS

You took off your purity ring because it was getting caught on her bra.
You know your relationship is in physical trouble. You knew what line you didn't want to cross—but it never even occurred to you that you could cross that line and more. By the end of the date, you temporarily lost all Christian, moral decision-making abilities. What you're doing is fun in the moment, but the next morning you feel guilty and a little dirty.

You've learned that Trojan is the name of something other than the USC mascot.
On the one hand, you think you'll never need condoms because you've decided not to have sex until you're married. On the other hand, all of your friends have been saying you should bring one along—just in case you need it.

You keep promising each other "this won't happen again."
You've had six talks in the past week and decided that you probably shouldn't have gone as far as you did. And now you're talking again tonight. This time it's different. This time you're serious. "We're not going to go that far again," you say....
   Starting tomorrow night.

SOLUTION

Know your reason for staying pure.
Your parents and youth pastor probably told you that sex before marriage is wrong. Maybe this admonishment kept you from having sex up to this point. But your parents and youth pastor may be hundreds of miles away now. You need to have your own reasons for staying a virgin or recommitting to purity before marriage. If you aren't sure about your reasons for staying pure, here are a few to think about.

- You're saving one of the greatest gifts you can give for your future mate.
- You're respecting God's design for sex within marriage and avoiding painful regrets.
- You're avoiding the guilt that having sex before marriage can cause, possibly trapping you in a relationship.
- STDs are unattractive.
- You'd like to graduate from college before having kids of your own.

You may have other reasons for why purity is important to you. So before you get yourself in a situation you might regret, remember those reasons. Then use those as motivation not to put yourself in a situation where your values may be compromised.

Get out of the relationship.
If it's clear that you're dating someone who doesn't respect you or keeps testing your boundaries, *get out of the rela-*

tionship! We're not sure how to put it more simply than that. If someone doesn't respect you or your values, then this person is most likely trying to take advantage of you.

Keep it in your pants and other boundary rules.

It's up to you to decide the answer to the age-old question "How far is too far?" We aren't going to say, "You can make out, but only for a maximum of 10 minutes," or "Don't go past first base after midnight."

We *can* tell you to remember the reasons for staying pure and to keep them in mind as you make this decision. Once you've decided, create specific rules for your relationship. Then talk about these rules with your honey bunny so you're on the same page. As you do, remember: The most effective rules don't go right up to the fence line, but keep a healthy distance away.

Don't worry about what everyone else is doing.

You have every right to make your own decisions about your physical relationship. Someone who's pressuring you to go further than you want to go might say, "We're the only ones not doing it." This simply isn't true. It's something desperate people say in the heat of the moment.

Try not to be alone together.

If you're having a difficult time not crossing physical boundaries, then don't be alone together behind closed doors. You'd be amazed what you won't do when there are screaming kids and chatty roommates sitting next to you.

Set a curfew.

One of the most practical solutions we can suggest is a self-imposed curfew. Many college students just *end up* alone together in the late hours, only to find the physical temptation too strong. Make a curfew hour that you can keep and don't break it. Too many mistakes happen after hours, and they're usually regretted for a very long time afterward.

Find a mentor to keep you accountable.

Find someone you can be honest with and tell that person about the lines you're trying not to cross with your special someone. It's much easier to keep your boundaries if you know a friend will be asking you about it.

> *Find someone who is stronger than you are—maybe even a little older than you.*

We recommend that you set boundaries because when you're in the heat of the moment, it's too easy for things to go in directions that you really don't want them to go. You may have strong convictions about your physical relationship, but these can be compromised in the name of love, hormones, or experimentation.

We're not giving you all of these rules to be the sex police.[4] We're doing it because as we've researched this book and worked with college students, we've seen the troubles and baggage that premarital sex can bring into a relationship. It can make a person feel trapped. It can cause un-

---

4. It turns out that the Sex Police is also the name of a washed-up punk/ska band.

necessary shame and guilt. It can damage self-worth. It can lead to unwanted pregnancies that can end college careers and forever alter a person's dreams for the future.

Like we said, the issue of refraining from sex before marriage is about respecting something God created—and that respect is good for your faith, your future spouse, and your own emotional well-being.

I GOT DUMPED FOR JESUS
DEALING WITH A BREAKUP

SITUATION

It was the best two months, one week, and three days of your life.

Everyone told you and your girlfriend, "You make the perfect couple." It was hard to disagree. She was the first girl you ever met who actually *liked* to watch action movies. You hate talking on the phone, but you could talk on the phone with her for hours. You laughed all the time whenever you were together. And after sitting through a crazy philosophy lecture, you couldn't wait until later when the two of you would grab some coffee, walk around campus, and you'd tell her all about it.

But one day she says, "We need to talk."

What does she mean we need to talk*?* you think. *Don't we talk all the time? Every day? Why does she suddenly* need *to talk?*

She launches into her speech, "I'm not ready to get this serious."

"We don't have to be serious," you say. "I can be very funny."

She doesn't even smile. She has everything she wants to say planned out, and she doesn't want you getting her off track. She then gives you one or more of the following clichés:

- "It's not you, it's me."
- "I really need to focus on school right now."
- "I'm a vampire."
- "I've met somebody else."
- "I have a fear of commitment."
- "I'm dating Jesus."

This last one is the absolute king grandmaster of all Christian breakup clichés.

You try to respond. "We can make this work," you say. You argue. You yell. And then she yells back.

Finally, you say, "It's okay if you date Jesus. But can't you date me *and* Jesus?"

She doesn't answer. She just kisses you on the cheek and walks off into the sunset and back to her dorm. You feel like you've been hit by a semitruck as you realize the unthinkable has just happened: The best two months, one week, and three days of your life are now over.

SYMPTOMS

Every song on the radio is about you.
You know you've been in a bad breakup when every song on the radio reminds you of your ex. You turn on your car and hear a song about a first kiss, and it reminds you of your first kiss. Maybe this song was even playing when you had your first kiss.

Next, a different singer shouts something like, "I will survive!" or "My life is so much better without you!" or "Next time you'll think twice before you cheat on me!" And you feel as though every one of these songs was written about you and your situation. Boy band songs that you used to hate now have this strong earth-shattering truth.

You picture how you'll get back together.
You imagine she'll call and say, "I've made the worst mistake of my life." You'll meet her at that coffee shop out on the pier overlooking the lake, and she'll beg you to take her back. "I think about you all the time," she'll say. You'll smile and say, "Nobody's perfect," and then you'll kiss her under the moonlight. Six months later, you'll be married.

At least that's how it plays out in your head.

You're on the rebound.
You have this urge to get in a new relationship as quickly as possible. You suddenly want to date people you'd never considered talking to before. It doesn't matter *who* you're dating—it just matters that you *are* dating. You want to get back in the relationship saddle as quickly as humanly possible.

You strategize how to win her back.
You never proved how much you cared about her the first time. So now you're willing to go to the extreme to prove your love. You write her songs. You have everyone in her chemistry lab bring her a rose—one by one—until finally you're standing there in the doorway holding a big poster

board sign that says *I miss you* surrounded by hearts. You're sure this grand gesture will win her back once and for all.

Either that or she'll think you're very creepy.[5]

SOLUTION

Process your feelings.

Find a friend with whom you can process what's happened. Talk about how you're feeling. Ask what went wrong. But whatever you do, don't bottle everything up inside. And don't try to process your feelings with the person who just dumped you. Don't call him up and ask to have one more conversation for the sake of closure. This will just depress you.

Get out of your room.

Don't stop living your life just because you had a bad break-up. Stay active. Join a sports team. Try out for the spring production of *King Lear*. Go out with a group of friends on Friday night. The more you live your life, the easier it will be to move on. Get out of your room and do something— even if you don't want to move on. We're not saying there's absolutely no way you'll get back together. But we are saying that you're not going to seem very attractive to anyone if you just sit in your room and listen to folk music while crying over pictures from your ski weekend in Vail.

---

5. If she thinks you're creepy, refer back to prerequisite 3. It offers some friendly reminders of how *not* to become the Stalker.

Put away the memories.
There may be reminders of her all around you. The teddy bear you won for her at the fair, the boxed set of Chuck Norris DVDs she bought for your birthday, the picture she drew of you, and the air freshener she bought for your car.

If these things are distracting, depressing, or reminding you of that special someone when you just need to get over her, then maybe it's time to put those keepsakes in a box. You don't have to throw them away or burn everything in a bonfire (although doing so can be surprisingly therapeutic). But at the very least, make sure there are no reminders of your old relationship in your car, your dorm room, or your shower caddy.

Don't rebound.
If you've been through a bad breakup, don't rebound and find someone new as quickly as possible. You're just going to dump this person, and then he'll do the same to someone else. Stop the vicious cycle. Don't rebound.

Get back in the saddle.
You may believe that your boyfriend was one-of-a-kind and you'll never find someone like him again. Okay, we've got to be honest here and say that you're probably right. But we can also say that you'll most likely find someone who's different and better than he was.

Relationships don't just end—they end for a reason. So take time to mourn it. And whenever you're ready get back out there, just be your charming self and start again with step one in situation 301.

PART (DANGEROUS SITUATIONS) 4

(PREREQUISITE 4: THREE TYPES OF COLLEGE PARTIES)

BEFORE YOU BEGIN READING "DANGEROUS SITUATIONS" …

YOU SHOULD KNOW ABOUT COLLEGE PARTIES.

We've hinted about college parties in some of the earlier situation descriptions. But, unfortunately, they're one of the most well-known parts of life on campus. Turn on any movie or TV show about college, and you'll probably see more scenes depicting parties than classrooms.

So let's explore them a bit further. There are many variations, but we've grouped the parties into three main types.

The first is what we'll call the Kegger. It's the most infamous type of the three. It's also the most popular and common. And the goal is for everyone to get as drunk or crazy as possible.

The second party doesn't have much of a goal at all, which is why it's called the What Do You Want to Do? party. Christian students usually wish to avoid the Kegger. We applaud this—students shouldn't get so drunk that they can no longer spell or even recognize their own names. However, many times this desire leads them to throw an alternative party that's best known for what it *doesn't* have because the goal is to avoid getting into any trouble. This is why the WDY-WTD party has no alcohol, very little food, and no real plan for fun.

Finally, there's the I've Brought You Here for a Reason party. Its goal is to recruit you or get you to participate in something.

We won't tell you what types of parties you should and shouldn't go to. That's up to you and your convictions. But this book is about survival, so we'll let you know where these parties hold dangers, how to spot them, and how to survive them.

So come on—let's party!

THE TYPES

THE KEGGER

The sights and sounds of the Kegger smack you in the face as soon as you walk into the place. In the kitchen a guy stands on his head and drinks straight from a keg as everyone cheers for him as though he's rushing down the sideline for the game-winning touchdown. In the living room, a DJ spins, and girls wiggle their hips with the ease of seasoned belly dancers. You walk past the bathroom and notice the bathtub is full of orange Jell-O, for some reason. And you're afraid to go upstairs because you can only imagine what's happening there.

Suddenly you realize: You've been to house parties before, but never one like this. College students have the house party down to a well-refined science. You stand in the middle of the walkway as people go back and forth, laughing and tickling each other and spilling the drinks in their red plastic cups.

You think to yourself, *How am I going to survive this?*

IDENTIFYING CHARACTERISTICS OF *THE KEGGER*

Also known as: Frat party, house party, rager

You'll observe: Kegs, cheering, togas, beer bongs, and a lack of coherent sentences

Locations: Sorority or fraternity house, a residence, a large yard, a field, an entire city block, a football stadium parking lot

Words you'll hear: Chug, wasted, hammered, I'm the Queen of Scotland

You'll be pressured to: Drink, drink while standing on your head, shout, dance, strip, dive into the swimming pool with or without your clothes on

You'll know the party's over when: The sun rises or the beer runs out

HOW TO SURVIVE *THE KEGGER*

If you're going to one of these parties, know that they're filled with dangers. Don't turn one night into something you'll regret for the rest of the semester, the year, or until you have college kids of your own.

Here are the steps to surviving the Kegger:

- *Go with a group of friends* — you'll be the safest in a group.

- *Don't accept a drink from someone you don't know.* At worst, a drink from a stranger could have something dangerous in it. Or maybe this stranger has really bad taste and makes drinks out of root beer, Tang, and Guinness.
- *Stay out of the kitchen.* The odds of having to contort your body and drink from a funnel jump dramatically as soon as you set foot in the kitchen.
- *Don't go off with someone alone.* He may seem like a nice guy. Let him prove it by giving you a call tomorrow.
- *Don't go into the basement wearing flip flops.* Few things are more disgusting than beer sludge on the floor — it's usually a mixture of old beer, mildew, dirt, and new beer.
- *Be yourself.* Don't feel pressured to do anything that makes you uncomfortable.

THE WHAT DO YOU WANT TO DO? PARTY

On the other end of the spectrum is the What Do You Want To Do? party. When you walk in, you'll immediately think you're in the wrong place. The apartment will be as quiet as a library, and the host will calmly say, "How are you?"

"Fine," you'll say.

And then there won't be anything else to talk about. You'll think, *This is the lamest party I've ever been to.*

Christian students often throw these types of parties and invite some people over. But no one has anything in common, there's nothing to do, and most likely there'll be very little food.

These awkward parties are safe, but they'll leave guests feeling ready to do just about anything to salvage a Friday night.

Parties without a plan often end up with everyone sitting around asking "What do you want to do?"

IDENTIFYING CHARACTERISTICS OF THE *WHAT DO YOU WANT TO DO?* PARTY

They'll have: No food, diet soda, a lack of music, conversations where everyone is using their inside voices

You'll observe: Not a whole lot

Possible locations: Apartments, basements, someone's parents' house

Statements you'll hear: "What do you want to do?" and lots of excuses to leave the party

You'll be pressured to: Think of something to do, or talk about what happened in your history class just to fill the awkward silences

You'll know the party's over when: It's 9 p.m.

HOW TO SURVIVE THE *WHAT DO YOU WANT TO DO?* PARTY

You may be kicking yourself if you've ever ended up at a WDYWTD party. It's Friday night. And there won't be another Friday *for a whole week*. But don't worry. There's hope. The party can still be brought to life. You could—

- *Play matchmaker.* Imagine yourself as eHarmony with legs. Get to know some of the girls and guys at the party. Find out their interests and then try to match a person with someone else. Say things like, "Dave, did you know that Marsha also likes kick boxing?" Once you've paired off some lucky young couples, sit back and watch what happens.

- *Turn on some music.* People are much less likely to talk when there's silence. Music + people talking louder = a more lively party.

- *Play a game.* There are lots of fun icebreaker games you can play, such as Mafia, Charades, and Twister. Too boring? Have some sort of food challenge. See who can drink an entire gallon of whole milk in an hour. Give everyone an Alka-Seltzer tablet and a swig of soda and see who can keep his mouth closed the longest. Have someone eat a handful of Pop Rocks and drink some soda to see if her head actually explodes. Good clean fun.

- *Crash another party.* You could invite everyone to go to another (more lively) party. Or just load everyone into a minivan and drive around town until you find a wedding reception or maybe a square dance at a retirement home. Everyone there will love your youthful enthusiasm.

THE *I'VE BROUGHT YOU HERE FOR A REASON* PARTY

Some parties have very clear goals. In fact, these goals are so stringent that the party cannot be swayed from its original intent. When you arrive, the host will smile, offer drinks and appetizers, and chitchat about anything and everything. Then suddenly the music fades. Everyone gets quiet.

"I've brought you here for a reason," the host says.

This reason could be anything. Sometimes the goal is to pair you up with another person of the opposite sex. If someone suddenly takes out a ketchup bottle, says words like *Truth or Dare,* or has you pull car keys or a driver's license out of a hat or bowl, then you know the goal for the evening is for you to hook up.

But there are many other reasons you could have been brought there. Perhaps the host whips out some makeup samples and wants everyone to have a makeover. Next thing you know, you're told how much money you can make by throwing parties just like this one and selling makeup—or clothing or life insurance policies or free-range chicken.

Either way, you've been brought here for a reason, and you have a feeling that you're not going to escape this party alive if you don't give in.

IDENTIFYING CHARACTERISTICS OF THE *I'VE BROUGHT YOU HERE FOR A REASON* PARTY

Also known as: Recruiting party, Mary Kay party, key party

Identifying characteristics: Nametags, props, chairs in a perfect circle, overly friendly hosts, elaborate costumes

Statements you'll hear: "What's your sign?" "This is going to be fun!" "Have you ever thought about being your own boss?"

You'll be pressured to: Participate — this could mean signing up to be a salesperson, hooking up, going around the circle and sharing your deepest fear, or whatever else the host has in mind

You'll know the party's over when: The host's goal for the evening has been accomplished

HOW TO SURVIVE THE *I'VE BROUGHT YOU HERE FOR A REASON* PARTY

Everything will seem focused as soon as you walk in the door. Maybe you'll be given a nametag. Maybe some of your friends or the host will try to pair you up with *someone who's perfect for you.* In any case you'll quickly realize you haven't been invited to party — you're being recruited for something. If you find yourself in this situation, you should —

- *Eat lots of free food.* The best thing about these IBYH-FAR parties is the free food. It's usually great. Some people will feel bad for eating it because they don't plan on signing up. But if you've been dragged to one of these parties, don't feel bad. Just go back for another one of those delicious mini éclairs.

- *Sneak out the back.* You can always leave. Just walk right out the front door or the back door; or—in an extreme case—climb out a window.
- *Don't sign on the dotted line.* A lot of these parties will have you sign up to buy or sell products. Or they'll have you hook up with someone before the night ends. Don't do it. A simple no will usually do. But if not, then move on to the next suggestion ...
- *Claim to have Irritable Bowel Syndrome.* This is an actual medical condition, and you should claim to have it only during absolute emergencies. But if someone is trying to pressure you to do something—sell products, hook up, and so on—then claim to have IBS as a last resort. If there's a host that just won't take no for an answer, talk about how irritated your bowels are. This is a surefire way to get a pushy host's attention off of you and onto someone else.

401

THE FRESHMAN 15
STAYING HEALTHY IN COLLEGE

SITUATION

Your parents bought you a meal plan that expires tomorrow.
You have a remaining balance in the amount of $289.35.
This balance is so high because instead of eating the cafeteria food, you've been eating out nearly every day and getting pizza or Chinese food delivered to your dorm room a couple times a week.

A campus convenience store near your dorm sells all kinds of snacks and junk food—and it also accepts meal plan cards. You think you might as well spend the remaining balance before it expires. You walk into that convenience store with two large rolling suitcases. It looks like you're robbing the place as you pack sodas, bags of chips, candy, and energy drinks into your bags.

On your way back to your dorm room, you run into Kyle Anderson, the guy you've been hoping would ask you out all semester.

"How are you doing?" he asks.

"Fine," you say. Then you notice him looking at the bags of food behind you. *This isn't me*, you think. *Really, I don't eat this much!*

You always seemed pretty healthy in high school. But now you don't know where all these extra pounds came from. You're not sure why you're eating so unhealthily and why just walking up and down the stairs makes you tired.

SYMPTOMS

Your midnight snack is the biggest meal of the day.
College is a busy time. We've established that. There are classes during the day, after supper you're off to the library to study and work on a group project, and then it's time for the midnight basketball game. Finally, it's late at night and you can't remember when you last sat down to eat a meal. You're starving, and it's past midnight. But now you don't have a curfew, and you know that Taco Bell is open 'til sunrise. You roll up to the drive-though window with some friends, order $20 worth of dollar-menu goods, and then eat them all before leaving the parking lot.

You feel like you have to get your money's worth every time you visit the buffet at the cafeteria.
Back home, going to an all-you-can-eat buffet was a once-in-a-while kind of treat. Nowadays, eating until your stomach hurts is an everyday occurrence. Your day revolves around meals. You can bring your textbooks, find a corner seat in the cafeteria, and make yourself an ice cream sundae with extra fudge while you study.

Your jeans shrunk three sizes in the wash.
That's the only excuse that makes sense. Otherwise, every time you put on your favorite jeans with the cool stitching, you're reminded of the weight and size you used to be. You

started by letting your belt out a notch after a meal, but now you've outgrown all the notches *and* the jeans. People told you about the freshman 15, but you never thought it would happen to you.

You keep hearing the term *stress eating*.
Your friends keep joking with you about stress eating, but there's a look of seriousness in their eyes. You're ready to give them a piece of your mind. You're ready to say, "Stop judging me!" In fact, you have a lot that you want to say to your friends, and you're going to say it just as soon as you finish your Twinkie. They're probably judging you for eating your third snack cake. But the only reason you're eating it is because Twinkies help you think when you have to write an American history paper. So as soon as you're done eating the Twinkie, you're going to say, "I'm not really stress eating. And even if I am, it's perfectly natural."

SOLUTION

Exercise
If you're like most incoming college students, you've never had to formally exercise before in your life. You somehow kept fit while pounding down the chips and soda because you were on the JV soccer team. Now that you're in college, exercise doesn't come as easily. You'll soon learn that your metabolism isn't what it used to be.

Most colleges have world-class gyms that are free for all the students to use. It just takes a little discipline and ambition to make your way across the campus. Schedule a couple of times a week to exercise and stick to the schedule. If you're not disciplined enough to do this (most of us aren't), then find a friend to go with you. You'll feel much better leaving the gym than the buffet line. While college is no doubt a stressful time, exercise has been proven to decrease stress much more effectively than stress eating.

Be aware of what and when you're eating.

Many college students eat the majority of their food late at night and in very large quantities. We're not doctors, but we're sure this can't be healthy. (If it helps, all the doctors we've talked with have also said this isn't healthy.)

Stop and think about the habits you're forming. Are you stressed all day and then eating all evening while you study in your dorm room? If you mindlessly snack on cookies while doing your biology homework, you'll have no idea how many you're actually eating.

Some college students keep a food journal of everything they eat in a day. There are programs online that can help you count your calories. Or online food journals are just a Google search away. Use these tools. Upon reviewing the week's food intake you might be surprised by what you're eating (junk food and gallons of soda) and what you're not eating (fruits and vegetables). These are tools designed to help you develop healthy eating habits. And if you have a history of eating disorders, please see the note at the end of this chapter.

Fast

The spiritual discipline of fasting is a powerful experience. Fasting is simply going without something—most commonly food—for a certain period of time. There are no universal rules about fasting. Some people won't even drink juice during a fast, while others will blend or liquefy anything. Fasting is a way to say no to your body and yes to God. It's a great way to start breaking bad habits and refocusing your energy on spiritual growth. At the heart of overeating is the sin of gluttony. Overindulgence and reckless consumption is not just a physical problem; it could very well be a spiritual problem that needs to be dealt with head-on.

A Note on Eating Disorders

Eating disorders are pandemic on college campuses. A healthy life and healthy eating habits are the goals of this chapter, not just losing weight. College is a time when extra stress and loneliness can manifest themselves into various types of eating disorders. If you have a propensity toward an eating disorder, *get help.* Tell someone you trust about your unhealthy struggles to look a certain way. You can also seek real help by talking to a counselor. Most colleges have professional counselors on staff who are willing to meet with students free of charge.

402

WHAT'S THE DIFFERENCE BETWEEN F AND F-MINUS?
TIME MANAGEMENT

SITUATION

You're stressed about the amount of work you've let pile up.
A few weeks into the semester, the unthinkable happens:
You're failing a class. And you have a D in another class.

How did this happen?

It probably started when you couldn't get anything done.
You always make plans to lock yourself in the dorm room
and get a serious amount of schoolwork done, but then
your roommate says, "You know what would be awesome?"
This question is usually followed by one of three statements: "If we converted the TV in the dorm lounge into a
3-D screen," "If we pranked the girls in room 207," or "If
we cooked some bacon on top of our wall heater."

How are you supposed to focus? You can't get anything
done in the dorm. So you go to the library and find it closed.
And in your favorite coffee shop some idiot with a guitar
is screaming songs about a girl named Sheila. *Where has
the day gone? Again?* How are you supposed to do better in
class tomorrow when you still haven't studied today? The
term *time-management* comes to mind, but you brush it
off, telling yourself, *I don't have time to manage my time.*

SYMPTOMS

You brag about pulling all-nighters.

You say things like, "I always do better on an assignment when I cram the night before."[1] The truth is that you're jealous of the people who've already done their assignments, and you secretly wish you could learn how to manage your time better.

You can't say no.

You have two midterms and a paper (which you haven't started writing yet) due tomorrow. Do you have time to play *Halo* with the fellas? Obviously not! But you don't want your friends to think you can't handle Legendary mode. If only you could learn to say no.

You bring flashcards to church and on dates.

Your whole life is consumed with completing assignments, passing tests, and getting good grades. You've brought your study cards to church in case there's some downtime between the worship time and the sermon when you can go over a few vocab words. And while your girlfriend is looking over the menu at dinner, you're memorizing the periodic table. You never seem to be totally there. Your mind is consumed with thoughts of all the other things you need to be doing, and you can't relax.

---

1. This statement is just an old college-student tale told by students everywhere.

Time spent on a college essay

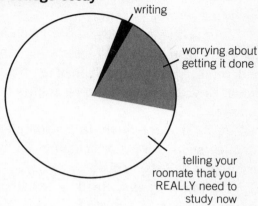

writing

worrying about getting it done

telling your roomate that you REALLY need to study now

SOLUTION

Change your study habits.
If you're like most college students, the increased load of homework and studying stretches your ability to manage time in ways you didn't think possible. In high school you could study during lunch and still pass a test in the afternoon.

College is different—your professors actually expect you to read the assignments and be able to remember everything that was talked about in class. You're going to need to learn to set aside large amounts of time to study and finish your assignments. If you're having trouble studying, here are some tips that will help you raise the grades in your classes or get scholarships.

We now present Rob and Joe's seven study habits for highly successful students:

1. *Turn off the TV.* Having the TV on in the background can really distract you. An interesting scene may come on, and you'll spend the next hour enthralled with the outcome. Or your attention will be split in half if you're trying to read.

2. *Find a place to study.* Have a place to go, such as a coffee shop, library, or computer lab where you can set aside time and stay focused.

3. *Study every day.* Reading assignments and working on papers is just a part of life for a college student. If you let it all pile up before midterms, you'll have a difficult time catching up. And even if you can catch up, you probably won't get the grades you want by cramming at the last minute. Carving out time every day to study and keep up with your classes will help you perform at a high academic level. And what's better than performing at a high academic level?

4. *Review your notes after every lecture.* Professors can throw a lot at you during their lectures. If you wait a couple of days, a week, or even a month to review your notes, then you may have no idea what they mean. Take some time after every lecture to reread your notes, highlight important facts, and get a better grasp on the information. You'll be more comfortable with the material when it's time to use it for tests and papers.

5. *Study in groups.* If you feel like your notes are incomplete, you can join a study group to help fill in any gaps.

Professors can move pretty quickly during lectures, but study groups can help you with the big ideas of philosophy and psychology. They can also help you break down difficult problems in your science and math classes. And you can help the other people in your study groups as well. Study groups are a great way to understand what's going on in your classes and make friends. Just make sure you're part of a study group that, you know, studies.

6. *Slay dragons first.* This just means you should start with your most difficult homework projects first. Do those assignments that seem the most daunting and overwhelming when you're fresh and full of energy. If you do the easier homework first, you'll just keep thinking about those dragons you still have to conquer. So get the harder stuff out of the way first so you can move on to your easier subjects. This approach will keep you from feeling overwhelmed in your more difficult classes.

7. *Take breaks.* College work is a marathon, not a sprint. Don't try to do all of your homework for five straight hours until you can't think straight. Homework doesn't turn out very well when you can't think straight. Do only as much as you can in one sitting, and then take a break. This may mean you do some homework in your room in the afternoon, get some dinner, play some foosball, and then go back to the library to join your study group or finish the rest of your work.

Learn to say no.
In college there's always something better to do than study a textbook. Scheduling time for fun and time for work is the key to time management. Turn the figurative key in the lock and keep to your scheduled times of work.

Sometimes that means saying no to *good* things. If you're the kind of person who says yes to every opportunity to volunteer or joins every group, you need to stop. College provides more opportunities than you've ever dreamed of. You might think that certain activities will be fun to try or look great on a resume—and they probably will. However, do you know what else looks good on a resume? Passing all of your classes! If these new responsibilities are keeping you from doing well in your classes, then it's time to cut out some things—no matter how painful it is to do. Think *school first ... then clubs and committees.*

Get tutoring.
In high school you may have thought of tutoring as being lame or unnecessary. In college, however, it's vital. You're dealing with much more complex material, and working with an upperclassman who knows the ropes can make at least a letter grade's difference. Imagine getting an A instead of a B or even a C or D instead of failing.

Reverse procrastinate.
This might sound crazy, but bear with us: What if you completed a project on the day it was assigned, instead of the night before it was due?

This is crazy, but it's crazy enough to work.

While other students spend the entire semester worrying about getting the assignment done, you've finished it during the first week of class. Imagine the joy you'll feel when you can call fellow classmates the night before the due date and torture them by asking what they're doing. Besides this fun, you'll also have more time to review your work and add creative details that won't come to you during an all-nighter.

Talk to your professors about extensions and getting more time to complete projects.

Be honest and let your professors know the legitimate reasons why you won't be able to make a due date. It'll go a long way. However, it also requires planning ahead. If you show up the day after an assignment was due and try to cry yourself into some extra time because you accidentally forgot about it and slept through your alarm, expect little sympathy.

Connect with your professor at least a week before a due date or final to tell him why you need more time. Be honest and let him know you'll be out of town or that you're feeling overwhelmed by the workload. Ask if there's any room for extensions. Professors will typically be sympathetic when they see that you want to do your best and you're putting in the effort. Most schools require professors to take a student's stress level seriously. If a student genuinely uses phrases such as *mental breakdown, panic attacks,* or *loss of sleep*, you can bet that student will receive some grace on the assignment.

Take a day off and rest.
You probably never thought that taking a day off could be a solution for time management issues. However, if you're always rushing around and running late, then something is wrong with the rhythm and flow of your life.

The Bible doesn't just recommend a day off—it commands it![2] It may seem impossible to imagine taking a day off with tests, group projects, and dreaded morning classes looming. But if you're really struggling with time management, this may be the best piece of advice you'll ever receive.

Taking a day off each week makes the rest of the week more strategic for doing your work. You'll find it easier to say no to watching the original *Star Wars* trilogy the night before an exam if you know you can just wait and watch it on your day off when you can truly relax while Luke Skywalker finds his destiny.

Your day off should be a full day spent recuperating from the week. It's a day for important stuff like God, church, friendships, and family that will give you the strength to go out and work like a dog for another six days.

---

2. This is commandment number four, for those of you who are counting.

403

I'M RICH—
I GOT A CREDIT CARD!
CREATING A BUDGET AND
STAYING OUT OF DEBT

SITUATION

"All you have to do is apply."
This is what the guy behind the credit card table tells you.
And if you apply, you'll get a free T-shirt and necklace. This
is too good to be true. For your whole life you've always had
to pay for T-shirts, but this guy is just *giving* them away.

So you apply.

No big deal, right? It's not like you're actually going to
use the thing. In fact, after you apply for the credit card,
you forget all about it. Until a couple of weeks later when
you go to your campus mailbox and find a letter from the
credit card company. You were *approved.*

That word looks so sweet: *Approved.* It means you're
worthwhile—you're trustworthy. Then a bright, shiny card
falls out of the envelope and into your hands. The letter
says you have a $10,000 credit limit. That's a lot of dol-
lars. You suddenly feel rich and powerful. Maybe you'll buy
a new car or treat your friends to a fancy dinner at a restaurant where all the waiters wear tuxedos. Why not? With the
credit limit you have, there's nothing you can't do.

A credit card doesn't mean you need to eat every meal at a five star restaurant.

SYMPTOMS

Everyone comments on your new wardrobe.
You don't work at a hip, fashionable clothing store—in fact, you don't have a job at all. But that doesn't stop people from commenting on your new clothes. You'll hear things like, "Nice jeans." "Where did you get those shoes?" "I didn't even know they made hats like that!"

This upgraded wardrobe is a result of your new credit card. Even better, when you went shopping, you learned you could also get a store credit card *and* 10 percent off your first purchase. So you went around and got new credit cards from all of your favorite stores. This is too easy!

You have five emergencies a day.
Your credit card spending is getting a little out of control. So you make yourself a promise: *I'll use this card only if it's an emergency.* The problem is that emergencies keep springing up. There's a concert that all of your friends are going to, and you have to go, too. You need to buy plane tickets for your spring break trip, and you also need a new swimsuit for said trip because wearing your current swimsuit would be a total embarrassment. But after those emergencies are taken care of, you're putting the credit cards away.

And you mean it.

Expenditures on a college "Emergency-Only" credit card

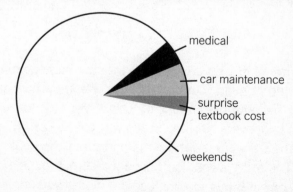

You learn new terms like *credit rating, interest rates*, and *minimum payment*.
You were just getting used to all of these new college terms, such as *blue book* and *midterm*. Now the credit card companies are mailing you minimum payment bills. *That's the minimum!* you think. Then they start calling you once you can't make the minimum payments anymore. This is less fun.

You get declined for every credit card you apply for.
You want to get some new credit cards to help you pay off your current credit cards so you can get everything back in order. You've learned your lesson about overspending, and now you just need one new credit card to consolidate everything.

But all of your credit cards have messed up your credit rating. Now you can't get this new consolidating credit card loan. What is the matter with these people? Don't they realize you're trying to fix the problem?

SOLUTION

Throw all of your credit cards into the homecoming bonfire.
You don't need your credit cards. We know how quickly you can become dependent on them. We also know how they can take over your life. That's why you're reading about this in the Dangerous Situations portion of the book.

The truth is you don't need a credit card. One of the best lessons of life is you don't spend money you don't have. And don't create emergencies for yourself. There will be other spring break trips. You get the idea.

Create a monthly budget.
Some simple steps to creating a budget:
1. Write down all of your income for the month, including work-study payments and paychecks.
2. Start by saving 10 percent and tithing 10 percent. Tithing is the practice of giving away a tenth of your earnings as an act of faith in God. You may believe that tithing is only for grown-ups, but tithing is about giving. The Bible calls us to be faithful and cheerful givers to our church and those in need.
3. Know all of your fixed expenses—car payments, insurance, and cell phone bill.
4. Write down the amount that's left over *after* you've paid your fixed expenses. That's called your "spendable income."
5. Designate categories for your spendable income and how much you can spend on each category. Think food, clothes, pet hamsters, and so on.
6. Stay within your budget.

We know budgets aren't the most exciting things to read about. It was a lot more fun when we were writing about frat parties and how to get a smoking hot girlfriend or boyfriend. However, this book is about surviving—and being successful. Following a budget is critical to your success now that you're living on your own. If you stick to this one, trust us—you'll be way ahead of most other college students.

Get out of debt.

Don't create a mountain of debt before you get out of college. One of the main goals of your education is to set yourself up to be successful when you graduate. And debt couldn't be more counterproductive to this goal. You don't want to have lots of debt because all of the money you're making at your great new job will go toward paying off credit card bills. And you don't want to have a lot of debt before you get married. Nothing is less romantic than saying, "Sorry, we can't take that honeymoon trip to Maui because I've got to keep up with my credit card payments."

If you have credit card debt, start making extra payments on the smallest bill until you get it paid off. Then make extra payments toward the next largest bill and so on. Keep doing this until you dig your way out of debt.

I TURNED ON THE COMPUTER, AND ONE THING JUST LED TO ANOTHER

DEALING WITH THE TEMPTATIONS OF PORNOGRAPHY

SITUATION

It's Saturday afternoon in your dorm room.
It's time to work on your biology homework, but you can't stay focused. Biology just isn't keeping your interest today. You like dissecting frogs, but learning about the genus and species isn't that interesting. Not on a Saturday, anyway. So now you're trying to find a way to procrastinate.

Then you do something you never do . . . you check your junk mail inbox. Inside, there's a note from Molly666. She writes, "I think you're cute. Come check out my site."

A voice deep down inside of you says, *This is a bad idea. Do* not *click on Molly666's Web site!* But your fingers aren't listening to that voice, and the next thing you know—you've clicked on the site. You feel guilty because of what you see, but now that you're here, you can't seem to stop.

SYMPTOMS

Before you let someone sit at your computer, you always delete the Internet history.

You feel ashamed of the sites you've been to, and you try to cover your tracks. Whether or not there's anything questionable in your recent Internet history, you have the overwhelming fear of being found out as the guy or girl who views pornography.

People know you as the "That's what she said" guy.

Your mind is so full of sexual thoughts that you respond to every conversational sentence with "That's what she said." Someone might ask you what you did today, and you respond, "That's what she said!" It's funny and makes perfect sense in your mind, but the person you're talking to doesn't even smirk. You're beginning to wonder if you might be the one with the problem.

Being alone in your dorm room is like a world war—you against the computer.

You have an immense desire to stop viewing pornography, but the temptation to keep looking is so strong. You pace the room, open and shut the door, and glance back at the computer. You know you can't sit down or else you'll give in to temptation. So you're left standing in front of your computer—just waiting for a miracle to stop the freight train of lust that's about to hit you.

Your roommate asks, "Why do you have so much hand lotion?"

As you look at your life, there are clear physical signs of your new habits. More than just the physical signs—such as purchasing large amounts of hand lotion—you're also spending more and more time withdrawn from the real world and off in your own little world of fantasy as you engage in what this book will refer to as *self-stimulating activities.*

SOLUTION

Step 1: Decide that enough is enough.

The normalcy of college guys and girls struggling with pornography shouldn't condone the activity. Anyone who's overcome an addiction will tell you that the journey to freedom started with a decision—a real decision to end the addiction. Habitually viewing pornography should be called what it is—an addiction. Come to the conclusion that you really want to stop this habit and move to the next step.

Step 2: Let the secret out—admit to the problem.

Sins done in secret can't be dealt with in secret. The trap of this addiction is being too ashamed to tell anyone. The more you hide it, the further you dig yourself into a pit that you can't get out of.

Many people find help through accountability. Accountability is often thought of as a cultish practice where people sit around and whip each other for the sins they've committed. Not so. Accountability can be as simple as letting a friend know how you're doing in an area such as viewing pornography. Giving someone permission to ask about your day or week is something that can help a lot of people bring their secret lives into the open for healing.

There's even a plethora of built-in filters on your Internet browser, as well as accountability software (such as covenanteyes.com or x3watch.com) that can help curb the temptation and strengthen the accountability process.

Once again, don't be ashamed to tell someone. Secrecy is the trap.

Step 3: Be willing to do whatever it takes.

With the easy accessibility of Internet pornography on nearly any electronic device, it's going to require some serious changes to your lifestyle to end this addiction. Are you willing to get rid of your computer or smart phone? Are you willing to leave your bedroom door open all the time?

Step 4: Get real help.

You don't have to fight this battle alone. There are groups out there to help you face this struggle. Contact your pastor, dorm director, or a Christian counselor and ask if they can recommend any groups or counselors who are specifically trained to help people overcome the addiction of pornography.

Your initial reaction to this step might be to think that it's going a little overboard to join a group for sex addicts just because you've been looking at some porn. But it's not. There are many groups of like-minded, college-aged Christians who meet together to get help. Anyone in these groups will tell you how problems of sexual addiction can grow out of the pornography gateway. Those people can also tell you about the freedom they've found that they didn't think was possible before joining a group like this.

PART 5

(ELECTIVES)

GOING GREEK

I don't even know how to spell "Pi Kappa Alpha."

WHAT IS A FRATERNITY OR SORORITY?

Fra-ter-ni-ty and So-ror-i-ty

It's a local or national organization of students that exists primarily for social purposes with initiations and rites and a name composed of two or three Greek letters. Fraternities have a definite reputation. If you tell your parents you're thinking about joining one, they may picture togas, kegs, and Will Ferrell streaking. And to some extent it's true that those types of fraternities and sororities do exist.

But in a fraternity, you can also build friendships, network, and do charity work. The key to joining one is to *know* as much as possible before you join.

To help you decide whether fraternity or sorority life is for you, we'll take you through the process of joining one and the pros and cons of Greek life.

IF YOU'RE THINKING ABOUT JOINING

Step 1: Decide if it's right for you.

Life in a fraternity or sorority isn't for everyone. So seriously think about whether you even want to start the process. (Read "The Good and the Bad" section to help you decide.)

Step 2: Learn more about the fraternities or sororities on your campus.

There are a few ways to do this. You can ask student services or other students and friends on campus about what's out there. When you're starting to learn more about the Greek houses, be sure to ask about their personalities and reputations. This information will really help you in your decision.

Step 3: Sign up to rush.

Rush week is the time when you can visit all of the potential fraternities and sororities on campus. We're not sure why they call it "rush week." But don't worry—you won't have to run at any time during this week. Many times you just choose the houses you want to visit and go to the scheduled parties.

Step 4: Visit the houses.

You can research all you want, but the best way to understand what's right for you is to visit the house. Decide if you'd fit in there—if you'd even *want* to fit in there. And ask the fraternity and sorority members some questions, such as, "What's the personality of this house?" "What sort of charity work do you do?" and "What are you best known for?" The answers will help you figure out which place best suits you.

Step 5: Put your game face on.

You're basically auditioning when you decide you want to join a fraternity or sorority. This may make you feel a little queasy (for a variety of reasons). But don't let it. There are many times in life when you have to try your best. You had to put your best foot forward just to get into college. You'll have to do it again to get a job. And honestly, you're going to have to try your best to impress your future spouse. So don't look at this as just a daunting task where you'll be judged. Look at it as a chance to step out and show everyone how awesome you are.[1]

Step 6: But don't put on someone else's face.
Rush is a time for everyone to get to know you—*you* being the key word there. Don't pretend to be someone else just so you can get into the house. Don't be the guy who loves foosball or the girl who loves to get pedicures if that's not the truth. Be yourself. Because that's who you're going to have to be whenever you're with this group of people for the next four years.

Step 7: Read the fine print.
There are tasks and chores you'll have to do if and when you become a pledge. This will be part of your initiation. So ask around. Find out what sorts of things you'll be asked to do. Members may be up front about some things, while other things might be a little more secretive.

Step 8: Pray.
After rush week ends, everything will be out of your hands for a bit. The Greek groups will decide who they want and

---

1. Because let's face it, you *are* awesome.

then issue their invitations to join. You may get invited to join the house you really wanted. You may not. Because this process is out of your hands, pray, trust God, and know you're going to be all right even if you don't get into the house you really wanted. There are more Greek letters in the sea—or something like that.

Step 9: Pledge.
If you get selected into a fraternity or sorority, you'll have to pledge. This mostly means you'll spend your freshman year being the lowest on the house totem pole, doing chores, helping upperclassmen, and getting initiated into the group.

Step 10: Join and make the most of it.
If you survive pledging and get to join the house, you'll have the chance to make some incredible friendships and impact lives. So have fun, be honorable, and make a difference in the lives of those around you.

THE GOOD AND THE BAD

You're still not sure if you want to join? Fair enough. To help you make your decision, we've listed "The Good" and "The Bad" about life in a Greek house. "The Good" lists reasons to join. "The Bad" lists reasons to run for your life.

You're in college now.

You must decide.

THE GOOD

You'll always have a place to fit in.
Life with frat brothers and sorority sisters means you'll have a place to sit at the basketball games (many times the group reserves seating), someone to eat with, and a group to call your own.

You'll have a place to hang out with like-minded people.
In the dorms, it's a crap shoot (as in the dice game) as to who you'll end up rooming with. But in a Greek house, you'll have a pretty good idea of what type of people you'll be hanging out with because of the rush week and pledging process we just walked you through.

You'll have support.
One of the most difficult things about being away from home is being away from family. It's easy to feel isolated and like you don't have a home base. It's easy to feel like there's no one to call when your car breaks down and you're stuck somewhere. Being in a Greek house means you have brothers or sisters to look out for you.

You'll never be bored.
Life in a frat house can be crazy. But it'll never be boring. So if you're the type of person who likes to drink 15 sodas and play foosball at 3 a.m., no problem.

You'll have friendships that will last long after college.
Fraternities and sororities are known for their parties. But what we found, after talking with former Greek members, was that the friendships were the most important thing about the experience. Being part of a community, such as a fraternity or a sorority, helps you form friendships and network with people who can help you out in your career later in life.

THE BAD

Pressure

There's a good reason why we told you to read the fine print regarding what you'll be asked to do after joining a fraternity. For most of your life, the people who are in authority over you have been telling you things to keep you out of trouble. But when you're a pledge, your new authorities (upperclassmen) may tell you things to get you into trouble. For instance, they can tell you to break into the zoo and give the polar bear a hug.

You'll say, "Are you sure?"

And they'll say, "Trust me. It'll be very funny."

When pledging to a fraternity, you maybe asked to hug a polar bear.

Time commitment

College already loads more responsibilities, homework, and social obligations onto your plate. And entering a Greek house will increase your responsibilities even more. You'll have social gatherings to attend, alphabets to memorize, parties to go to, and weekly chores. So if you're not great with time management (see situation 402), then Greek life might not be for you.

Hell Week
Your final rite of passage will be Hell Week. And, yes, it's called "Hell Week" for a reason. If you still decide to join—good luck.

You'll distance yourself from other friendships.
Sure you'll have a place to belong, but you'll also find it more difficult to build friendships outside of your frat or sorority—especially during your freshman and sophomore years.

Dues and other costs
There are usually dues involved in joining a fraternity. With all the other costs of college—room, board, books, and more—this can be another expense that you may not be able to afford. And it may be difficult to talk your parents into helping with this expense. Your mother may say, "There's no way I'm paying dues so you can go streaking through campus." This means you'll have to cover the costs yourself—which may mean getting a part-time job. Now you have even less free time.

THE DOS AND DON'TS OF DECORATING A DORM ROOM

Your room at home is something you've built over time. You went from displaying Barbie posters to Hannah Montana posters to some cool black-and-white prints of the Eiffel Tower. Only now you have to start over. New beds, all new layouts—and you're sharing it with someone you don't know. You haven't shared a room with someone since you were nine. So what are the dos and don'ts of decorating your dorm room?

DOS AND DON'TS

DO: *Go to Target*

You're going to need some new upgrades for your dorm room, so set a budget and go to Target, IKEA, or Anthropologie to get a new bedspread, desk lamps, and picture frames.[2] You'll want to display some pictures of your friends and family back home, and you may even want to leave a few empty frames so you can add some new memories.

DON'T: *Become Martha Stewart*

You want your dorm room to look nice, but you don't want to go overboard so that everything is overly matching and frilly and looks like Martha Stewart's house. Get simple

---

2. The authors of this book do not receive endorsement money from Target or any of these other stores. We just think they have cool stuff.

stuff that's nice and new. But not *too* nice because—and we're not sure why this is—the more expensive your bedspread, the more likely it is that someone will spill an entire two-liter bottle of soda on it.

DO: *Make your dorm room your own*
Your dorm room should reflect you, which means it's okay to decorate it with posters, photos, and vintage lamps that highlight your personality and interests.

DON'T: *Decorate your room with anything fantasy or sci-fi*
Listen, everyone loves Star Wars, Lord of the Rings, and Harry Potter. It's just that if you decorate your room with those things, you're going to get ridiculed. Take it from us. We had to learn this the hard way. And that goes for girls, too. Do *not* decorate your room with pictures of unicorns or anything Disney Princess. This will also be met with relentless scorn.

DO: *Plan ahead*
You'll want to know what sort of layout your room has and what size the bed is. And make sure to talk with your roommate about what he's bringing before buying lots of stuff for your new room.

DON'T: *Invest money and time without planning*
Before you buy that new bedroom set, you'll want to make sure it will fit in the space. Before you get that sweet, eight-person couch, you'll want to check to see if there's room for it. And before you get that cool new electric-blue-and-hot-pink lampshade/bed combo, you may want to see if it will clash with your new roommate's decor.

ELECTIVE 3

50 THINGS YOU MUST DO DURING YOUR FIRST YEAR OF COLLEGE

THIS CHAPTER IS ABOUT GOALS ...

Lots of them

The thing about goals is that if you don't set them, you'll never accomplish them. Setting goals enables you to think ahead and accomplish things you might not do otherwise.

So we've helped you by putting together a list of things you must do during your first year of college. Some of the checkpoints can be crossed off before you even get to college; some might require a whole year of being very disciplined. Some involve relationships (several with the opposite sex); others are about education. And still others are about things that will bring about the types of adventures you should have in college.

Use this list as motivation. As you check a goal off the list, you'll feel a grand sense of achievement that will carry you on to accomplishing the next one. If you can check off every one of these goals (or at least most of them) in your first year, you can consider yourself very brave.

Maybe even a little too brave.[3]

---

3. Okay, so we maybe got a little carried away with a few of these items. This will be a good chance for you to use the good judgment and responsibility we've talked about in earlier chapters. If any of these things seem like they might get you into trouble, make you unpopular, or get you arrested—you have our permission to skip them.

○ Don't put all of your eggs into one college basket. Apply to several schools just in case you don't get into your first choice.

○ Visit the school before deciding to spend four-plus years there.

○ Apply for 10 scholarships.

○ Pack for college.

○ Now unpack the unnecessary stuff. Don't forget that you'll be able to buy things when you get to college. You don't need to take along a year's supply of toilet paper.

○ Have one last good-bye party with your friends where you laugh and cry.

○ Contact your future roommate and discuss any furniture and decorations the two of you are bringing.

○ Get your own bank account and debit card.

○ Tell your parents you're going to be just fine at college.

○ At new student orientation, walk around the entire campus and collect all of the free stuff at the various booths—just don't sign any contracts.

○ Go to freshman orientation and play the game where you pass an orange from one person's neck to another. (Bonus points if you play that game with a baseball bat, Life Savers candies, or toothpicks.)

○ Meet with your guidance counselor and tell her about your plans for becoming a president or brain surgeon or just graduating in four years.

○ Introduce yourself by saying, "Hello, I'm Mr. (*your last name*)" to every person in one of your classes. Ladies, introduce yourself as "Miss (*your last name*)." You'll be amazed to see how people respect you when you introduce yourself as Mr. or Miss.

○ Spend a day going to your classes dressed as the school mascot. When your professor asks who's in there, make the universal "I don't know" mascot gesture.

○ Lay down some ground rules with your roommate about borrowing stuff, not cooking bacon in the room, or what hours it's cool or not cool to cook bacon.

○ Find a group of Christians and ask where they go to church.

○ If they don't have a church, vow that next Sunday the whole group will visit a new church every hour on the hour until you find a church you can call home.

○ Go to one fraternity or sorority party during rush week. Dress appropriately like a cowboy or in a toga. (Bonus points if you go dressed as a cowboy to a toga party or vice versa.)

○ Join a college club involving something you know nothing about—like the Hand Bells Club, the BBQ Grill Masters Club, or a club that reenacts the Battle of New Orleans or the War of 1812.

○ Visit a professor during office hours and ask, "How can I be you when I grow up?"

○ Serve at a homeless shelter during a holiday.

○ Get into a spiritual conversation with a student who disagrees with you.

○ Memorize Psalm 119.

○ Recite Psalm 119 in the middle of a casual conversation while out on a first date.

○ Read the Old Testament.

○ Guys: Ask out a girl by singing her a song you wrote just for her.

○ Girls: Write a song for a guy to sing just for you, and then hold a competition to see which guy gives the best performance of it. Agree to go on a date with the winner.

○ Go to a football game with at least one part of your body painted in school colors.

○ Stay standing for the entire game.

○ Wash your roommate's sheets. (This is the modern-day equivalent of the feet washing that Jesus did for the disciples.)

○ Have a heart-to-heart with your roommate about something that's bugging you.

○ Go on a mission trip for spring break.

○ Write a letter to your parents telling them how much you appreciate them.

○ Go to a party where the people are drinking alcohol and don't drink a drop.

○ Create a budget and actually keep track of your spending.

○ Start a food journal.

○ Use your food journal to cut back on all of the items that could cause the freshman 15.

○ Begin a new weightlifting routine and make sure to say things like, "Gotta work my quads now," throughout it.

○ Find someone who looks as lonely as you felt during the first week of college and ask that person to hang out with your group of friends on Friday night.

○ Pass all of your classes with a 3.3 or better.

○ Find all the requirements for five different majors.

○ Find all the requirements for eight different minors.

○ Meet with your guidance counselor again and use her name several times in the conversation to show your appreciation for all her help.

○ Give up something for Lent.

○ Go the entire year without streaking through campus.

○ If your friends insist on streaking, wear the school mascot costume and run with them while they streak. If campus security stops you and asks everyone, "Why are you streaking?" make the universal "I don't know" mascot gesture.

○ Resell all of your textbooks. (You'll never crack open these books again—trust us.)

○ Buy this book for an incoming freshman.

○ Make a list of 50 things that you wish were on this list.

○ Do those 50 things your sophomore year.

ELECTIVE 4

LETTER TO THE PARENTS OF COLLEGE STUDENTS

College students, we believe the following letter can be very helpful for your parents to read. If they haven't already read this section before they gave you the book, leave this book lying open to this page and sitting someplace where they'll find it. Good places include on their nightstand, near the coffee maker, or, if you must, in the bathroom.

FOR MOM AND DAD

Dear Parents,

The authors of this book wish to tell you something.

But first we want to tell you that there are parts of this book that you may think are too edgy for a Christian book, such as the sections on sex, alcohol, and pornography. Please trust us, however. These are the things that all college students deal with. Therefore, we took a somewhat humorous but truthful approach in broaching these edgy topics.

Okay, now that we feel better about ourselves, here's what you need to know. There's a question that all college students ask their parents. Yet, they rarely ask it with words but in the things they do to test you before leaving for college.

The question they're asking is Do you trust me? College students need to feel trusted. Let's face it, they're about to leave the nest, and the thing that will help them more than money, more than great advice, even more than those expensive textbooks is their parents' trust. Your son or daughter is probably going to mess up, probably going to call home feeling pretty lonely from time to time, and probably going to get a bad grade or two. But everything will be much better in your child's life if she knows you trust her. So please tell your college student that you trust her, and don't baby her or remind her a thousand times to do her homework.

The big idea is this: Parents, your role is now changing from disciplining to supporting your child. Stop worrying, she'll be just fine.

Sincerely,

Rob and Joe

P.S. Now that the heavy stuff is finished, here are some practical things that your college student will love:

- Don't ever call before 11 a.m. (noon on weekends).
- Send little care packages with homemade cookies and goodies.
- Clearly communicate about what you're willing and unwilling to pay for.
- Never surprise your child with a pop-in visit to the dorm. Always make plans to visit.
- Don't get mad if your child calls college "home" after a semester.
- If you're thumbing through this book in the bookstore, BUY THIS BOOK!

COMMENCEMENT
(SOME FINAL THOUGHTS FROM ROB AND JOE)

We hope this book was helpful.

We hope that if you found yourself on a nightmare date, you were able to open the book to situation 302 and figure out a way to survive it.

We hope that if you were assigned to live with one of the five difficult roommates, you didn't burn down your dorm just so you wouldn't have to deal with that person anymore. We hope you flipped to situation 106 instead and figured out a way to survive the semester. Maybe the two of you are even friends now. Maybe you're going to room together again next semester. Is that too much to ask? At the very least, we hope that situation 106 helped you figure out ways to be friendly when you pass each other on campus.

And even though college can be a time when students are challenged in their faith, we hope that reading this book helped you grow in your faith and connect to a church.

Still, you may be asking *Are these* all *of the situations I'll face in college?*

No. They are not.

And there are a couple of reasons for this:

1. This is supposed to be a situational handbook, not a situational encyclopedia.

2. We've shown you the main types of situations you'll face. But there are many variations.

For instance, in situation 101 we told you how to choose a college based on the typical criteria of cost, location, and education. But what if you're trying to choose the best Christian college? Or the college with the best sports team? Or the college where you have the best chance of finding your future spouse?

We told you in situation 402 how not to fail a class. We gave you the practical steps to survive. But we didn't tell you what to do if the unthinkable happens—if your dog *actually does* eat your homework. (We're not really sure what to do if that happens.)[1]

But we are sure about a couple of things. Whenever there's a situation that you don't have an exact answer for, follow these guiding principals:

- Don't do things you'll regret—like build up credit card debt or mismanage your time and fail your classes.
- Always use common sense. If the voice inside your head whispers, *I think this is a bad idea*—then it's probably a bad idea. So listen to that voice.

On the other hand, we're sure you'll encounter most of the situations in this book as you go forward into your first year of college and beyond. Honestly, that's a good thing because

---

1. Our best guess would be to tell the truth and bring in your shredded homework. However, your professor might not believe that, so seriously try to keep your dog away from your homework.

that means you're taking risks and putting yourself out there. It's okay to feel lonely—just don't stay that way. Do something about it. It's okay not to know what major to declare, but take some classes and find out what you're passionate about. The key is to get the most you possibly can out of your four years of college. And if it looks like you're going to need a fifth or sixth year of school, go back and reread situation 105.

You can't get through college without facing adversity in your faith, your classes, your friendships, and your other relationships. The key to college is to learn to overcome these problems and keep moving forward. You're going to make mistakes. You're going to take missteps in some of these situations. But when you do get back up and dust yourself off, make things right and move forward. Don't let any of these situations conquer you. Learn to overcome them because if you learn to overcome problems, then you're going to find a lot of success in your college life.

And if you can survive college, you can survive just about anything.

Or you can always get a job at a coffee shop.

After High School Flow-Chart

Go to college
4 years of studying
↓
Meet for group
projects →
↓
Graduate college
↓
Get a vanilla latte
on the way to your
dream job

at
Starbucks

Don't go
to college
↓
Work

ACKNOWLEDGEMENTS

ROB STENNETT

I'd like to thank all of the bad decisions I made in college that gave me the idea to write this book. I'd also like to thank Gloria Gildea for working so hard with us on these amazing illustrations; Josh Ayew-ew for his super sweet graphs; my agent, Chip MacGregor, for his belief in our book; Heather Campbell for her patience, thoughtfulness, and editorial insight; and Youth Specialties for their collaboration on this project.

JOE KIRKENDALL

I'd like to thank my wife for reading this book and laughing at some of the jokes—even when they weren't that funny. Aaron Stern, the college pastor of the 20-somethings ministry of theMILL, and the rest of theMILL staff—thanks for letting me steal about half your jokes and sermon illustrations for this book. My parents—thanks for being awesome and trusting me during my college years. John Crist—thanks for your help writing the section about joining a fraternity or sorority. You're one of the funniest guys I know. And God—the true Author of any good idea worth thinking about.

Share Your Thoughts

With the Author: Your comments will be forwarded to the author when you send them to *zauthor@zondervan.com*.

With Zondervan: Submit your review of this book by writing to *zreview@zondervan.com*.

Free Online Resources at
www.zondervan.com

Zondervan AuthorTracker: Be notified whenever your favorite authors publish new books, go on tour, or post an update about what's happening in their lives at www.zondervan.com/authortracker.

Daily Bible Verses and Devotions: Enrich your life with daily Bible verses or devotions that help you start every morning focused on God. Visit www.zondervan.com/newsletters.

Free Email Publications: Sign up for newsletters on Christian living, academic resources, church ministry, fiction, children's resources, and more. Visit www.zondervan.com/newsletters.

Zondervan Bible Search: Find and compare Bible passages in a variety of translations at www.zondervanbiblesearch.com.

Other Benefits: Register yourself to receive online benefits like coupons and special offers, or to participate in research.

ZONDERVAN®

ZONDERVAN.com/
AUTHORTRACKER
follow your favorite authors